40 DAYS AND 40 NIGHTS

One woman's quest to reclaim her creative mojo

Eleanor O'Rourke

FORWARD

My boyfriend left this morning.

Last night's dialogue:

"I can't believe you're going away for two whole months!"

"Not two months, maybe six weeks. I'll be back before you know it. And besides it'll give you a chance to write in peace".

"I hate peace!"

"But you love writing".

Today's inner dialogue:

I hate writing!

To be more accurate, I have a love-hate relationship with writing, but recently my ability to feel the love is sadly lacking. I have various strategies for dealing with this lack of love, but my two biggies are list making and carbohydrates. Sitting at my desk with a chocolate milk and a notebook, I ponder the big subject of creativity. These are my top ten thoughts.

1. Creativity is not art, it's energy. It's our life force.
2. This energy is in ALL of us, though we express it in individual ways. It may take a traditional form like music, poetry or dance, but it could also be expressed as spontaneous smiling on the subway, random acts of kindness or a brilliant solution to a problem at work.
3. If we link creativity to love, we get passion. This amps up the energy to give us sufficient fuel to keep going when things get tough.
4. Energy has to keep moving – if it isn't expressed, it can create blockages in our system.
5. These blockages cut off the flow, making us tired and depressed.
6. Depression leads to all kinds of addictions.

7. Creativity is the only thing that makes us truly happy.
8. Unexpressed or stifled creativity is the source of all our misery.
9. Thus creativity is simultaneously the cause of our pain and the cure for it.
10. If we could crack the code, thereby accessing and giving expression to creative energy, that would be a very good thing indeed.

Having done the list, I now turn my attention to the calendar (a superior list as it has vertical as well as horizontal lines). My boyfriend is correct, he is not away for two months, he's away for 47 days. Could I change my relationship with creativity from love-hate to love in this time?

How about 40 days? 40 is an archetypal number, so it has more power. It's the number of days Jesus spent in the desert and Noah spent on the water. 40 is a test. If we want to make a commitment to cracking a code, we need all the help we can get from the symbolic realm.

40 is also realistic. I'm usually suspicious of books and programs that promise to make you rich, thin or confident in a week, if you follow 3 rules, 5 secrets, 7 steps. Surely we're grown up enough to cope with double digits by now. Changing a habit is a journey of many choices, not a quick fix.

If your creativity is stuck, strangled, scared or sleeping, join me on this 40 day challenge to reclaim your creative power.

Love-hate to love.

Duality to singularity.

Forty days.

One big prize.

INTRODUCTION

D-day minus 7 days

If a journey of a thousand miles starts with a single step, it follows that a book of 40 chapters starts with a single word. Better make that word count.

"If" is a word of possibility, the beginning of a famous poem by Rudyard Kipling. Sadly, unlike Rudyard, I have no fabulous words to follow it with. Writer's block is a curse. I have pursued various curse-breaking options, none of which have yielded results, so in the interest of science and spirituality, I am now going to take drastic action.

Things I have previously tried...

Self-help books: My bed is surrounded by many neat stacks, like cairns by the side of the road. Apparently these piles of stones are supposed to memorialize people or events, so it's fitting that my paper ones signify an absence of any sort of event and the death of characters killed off before being fully formed. I am an abortionist - it's no wonder I can't sleep. Looking at them, I now realize I also have an "Amazon" addiction and appear to be single-handedly propping up the self-help publishing industry.

Creativity workshops: Last week after trawling the Internet looking for advice, I chanced upon THE workshop that would fix everything. Despite the fact that I have previously been seduced by the bullet points on the flyleaves of so many books, I am now seduced by the "silver bullet" points of the workshop blurb. I drive many miles into the New Forest beyond the reach of GPS and mobile phone technology, get lost in dense woodland, and arrive late at a small hotel full of positive, happy, creative people. Feeling distressed, exhausted and without a single creative bone in my body, there is an instant disconnect. I am now sulking about paying a lot of money to listen to chapter 3 of book 74 (third rock from the bed). Perhaps I need an astrologer, rather than a coach.

It's the Cosmos Stupid! Wow that feels better. I can blame it all on Mercury Retrograde. I love astrology. Add the *I Ching*, to one of my piles and place a new order to Amazon for tomes on numerology, runes and other ancient forms of divination. Feel very High Priestessy and consider searching websites for Celtic jewellery and crystals with special powers.

D-day minus 4 days

The planets are in correct alignment and I have still not written a thing. My insomnia is causing me to look slightly deranged. This seems to fit with the creative writer's persona, so I'm going to complete the look by adding interesting scarves, fingerless gloves and clothes that quite frankly could do with a bit of an iron. Perhaps I could take up smoking and somehow try to absorb the spirit of the Left Bank in the 1930s. If everything is energy (book 16 "rock" 4), then the molecules of F. Scott Fitzgerald and Ernest Hemingway are out there somewhere... I just have to Vis-ual-ise!!!

D-day minus 2 days

Visualization techniques require a meditative state, which is difficult to enter when surrounded by credit card bills requiring payment for the various accoutrements of the creative endeavor and electricity bills (you can't type with cold hands and those fingerless gloves are just ineffective). I sit with my friend Chloe who is in a similar desperate situation. She has just given up her day job in the hope that this flamboyant gesture will be rewarded with inspiration... "Trust the Universe!" (book 24 "rock" 5). She is also temporarily homeless (how bohemian) so is staying with me for a month until her flat share comes available.

After five cups of coffee and an entire box of chocolate brownies, neither of us have written a word. An advertisement cuts through the gloom of the empty laptop screen. British Airways are doing last minute discounted flights to France! I mean really, if you can't be creative in France, you can't be creative anywhere. We sign up and five minutes later, secure a hire car and a cottage, one hour's drive from Perpignan.

D-day

Actually feel creative while eating breakfast. Start writing for the first time in weeks – a romantic comedy about a new-age girl and a geeky science boy who meet in an airport lounge. Chloe is in similar mode, frantically scribbling details of an extraordinary dream before it escapes her grasp and disappears back to the underworld. The numbers on the clock at the top corner of my laptop seem significant, but my right-brain, having finally decided to play, is now engaged in a flurry of activity. Half an hour passes before I realize we should have left for the airport...

Rock 4 (not the cheese but equally effective in keeping you up half the night)

DAY ONE

Wake up in France. "Wake up" implies having previously been asleep, so perhaps "sit up and reach for the laptop" would be more accurate. I'm still not sleeping. A frustrating journey didn't help. The usual airport malarkey. The long queue for the rental car, at the end of which we realize that I've forgotten my driver's license and Chloe's credit card won't work, and that apparently two halves (her license and my card) don't make a whole.

Eventually, with monies transferred, paperwork completed and additional sale items avoided, we pick up the smallest car in the world. It looks nothing like the Peugeot we were promised - the words "or similar" having much artistic license in the world of Hertz.

Meanwhile, in the land of inspiration, the muse has evaporated. Finding the romance in travel these days would require more than "creative mind" stimulation, it would necessitate complete suspension of "logical mind." Paradoxically, this state also renders you incapable of actually getting anywhere.

F. Scott Fitzgerald would never have this problem. He would drive a Bugatti on near empty roads, stroll on the deck of an ocean liner, white scarf flapping, moleskine notebook in hand. The skies he flew in would actually be friendly; they wouldn't need the services of an advertising agency to make them appear so. And can you imagine Ernest Hemingway's response, if asked to remove his shoes and belt? As for the double barrel shotgun under his arm, that doesn't bear thinking about. Security personnel would become an endangered species. And not before time.

Perhaps this is the core of the creative block. As the world becomes increasingly complex and frustrating, we feel we have to become sharper and more focused in order to survive. We gird our loins and fight a battalion of petty irritations before facing the archenemy (the one guarding our treasure trove of creativity) and wonder why we have no energy left.

In addition to this, time is our most precious commodity. Mistakes are costly, not just in financial terms. Creativity requires the implementation of hundreds of small choices – which idea/phrase/brushstroke to keep and which to kill? We need the luxury of being able to make mistakes so that we can hone our decision making capabilities and become more fluid in the capturing process. The mantra here is "choose, fail, recover, choose again" not "choose, agonize, hesitate and seek approval." When we take away the fear of failing, we get quicker with our choices, plus we are more likely to notice the jewels in the wreckage.

Back to my current surroundings: Photographs and description of this "cottage" on the website are completely misleading. The entrance is a garage front door and our maisonette is sandwiched in a dark, airless space between the garage and a small courtyard (very pretty in the photograph, as taken at an inventive angle that doesn't include all the recycling bins of the main house). There is a building site next door, so the imagined melodic sounds of rural France are replaced by the bleeps of reversing trucks and the churning of cement mixers.

No wonder creativity is in short supply. It's been captured by the dark side of capitalism, locked in a tower and forced to spin hyperbole for the Barons of Sales and Marketing.

I start typing. My target is 2000 words per day. It would help if I knew what story I wanted to tell, and if I didn't feel so tired. Ironically, in light of the previous few weeks, the urge to write a self-help book appears through the haze. A self-help book that could actually help normal people! A book that gets the left-brain and the right-brain to get on with each other and work as a creative team.

Come to think of it, that's not the worst idea I've ever had.

How to start?

Left-Brain versus Right-Brain...

I've got an idea for a book. It's coming. I can feel it...

THE DUEL (Who will be the first to die?)

In writing the opening of my new book, I must keep remember that high drama is not usually a feature of self-help manuals.

Here goes... The world comprises good things and bad things. Happiness and sadness. Hope and pessimism. Hot and cold. Light and dark. Left and right. Logic and Intuition. This is our world of duality.

Some man-made things are beautiful (St Paul's cathedral) and some are ugly (urban traffic signage). Some natural things are beautiful (mountains and flowers) and some are ugly (viruses and mosquitoes).

The things we think are good and bad may not be the same things that others think are good and bad. They are just our preferences. Our creative mind (right-brain) conjures ideas with many consequences. Our logical mind (left-brain) makes choices according to our preferences.

It follows that if we are to function well in this world of duality, and make good choices, we need a fully functioning "dual" brain – one that gives an equal voice to its left and right side. But how will we decide where the center point is between the creative and the logical? Is there some sort of tool that could enable this to happen? How will we expand our mind to create space for a multitude of ideas, instead of limiting ourselves to the tried and tested preferences?

I've got to come up with a multi dimensional tool. One that would increase our capacity, while focusing our choices; one that would manage the tension between the head and the heart; one that would establish a balance between left and right. How about...

A slide rule?
Rules imply rigidity - too left-brain and two-dimensional.

A spirit level?
Spirit is good, but "level" implies something static. Static things aren't creative. Also two-dimensional.

What we need is an internal GPS that allows for multiple adjustments – left/right, up/down, forwards/backwards, expansion/contraction. Something that allows us to know where we are at any given time so that we can make constant small adjustments in order to stay on track. Or of course go off the beaten track if we choose to embrace the "mistake" of a road less travelled.

I stare out of the window at the little car, barely visible behind the recycling bins and smile.

A Sextant (navigational tool used by old sea dogs)
Multi dimensional (check). Used for celestial navigation (yay, help from the cosmos). Works in the dark (convenient for late night trysts with the muse). Plus, tenuous link to the drama of piracy.

Brilliant.

I will write a book called *The Sextant*. A book that incorporates a tool to help normal people live a creative life.

First hurdle - the need to define "normal."

I will write a book for people like me. You know who you are. You have the same books by the side of the bed, the same frustrations and the same best intentions. Look at you. You're smart. You're sitting on a bundle of untapped creativity. You've got more potential than you can shake a stick at. Now look at the world. It needs you...

How small is this car?

DAY TWO

Self-help adage No. 2 **All experiences are meaningful and meaningless**

What would be the significance of finding ourselves in a horrible cottage after a journey that could only be described as frustrating and tedious? Positive thinking books would advocate an "attitude of gratitude." Find the positive in every experience. Is it just me, or does this make you want to kill with your bare hands?

I know, I know. It's not as if I've been hit by a plague of locusts. I don't exactly require the reframing skills of Job to realize that things could be a lot worse, but really! Sometimes positive thinking is delusional and allows others to keep on getting away with stuff that shouldn't be allowed.

Is there any way around the overselling phenomenon? Before I decided to embark on a career as a writer, I worked in the advertising industry. This is a world where people dedicate their lives to finding the positive aspects of the brands they promote, while remaining the most deeply cynical people on the planet. They can do this because they're often creative, intelligent, and funny, so the irony is not lost on them. They live in the heart of this paradox and the heart of anything, as it's so close to the center, is a good thing.

Whilst in advertising, I saw a constant influx of the latest graduate recruits, all desperate to work long hours, doing the most mundane of jobs for the chance to eventually rise to the ranks of copywriter or account director. The C.V.'s of these people were often the most creative thing about them. Having read *Brand Me* or whatever the latest business self-help book was at the time, they had repositioned themselves beyond belief.

It doesn't help that most of us were raised by fearful parents in a time of economic uncertainty. Creativity demands risk and pain - often new ideas don't work and that can be painful. How painful, depends on the flexibility of the people around us. As a young child our early endeavors were probably met with disapproval (re-pointing the kitchen tiles with strawberry yogurt isn't always appreciated by exhausted parents). School years are frequently marked by ridicule (how hard can it be to throw a javelin? – quite hard apparently). And adolescence is just another word for ritual humiliation. No wonder we find it hard to take risks and be creative.

Betty Edwards calls creativity "a different way of seeing", something many people lose around the age of ten when their left-brain becomes dominant. Drawings done around this age show the shift from free to narrow expression, from right to left-brain. Primary school children fill the whole page with color and shapes, without any need for editing. Secondary school children want things to look realistic so they focus on details. If their subject matter is a racing car, they will spend ages faithfully depicting the alloy wheels, while completely ignoring the background or the overall composition of the scene.

The ten year old's desire for realism (i.e. wanting the drawing to be "right" trumps the allowing of imagination. Thus the world of duality (right and wrong) gets embedded. When children can't achieve sufficient realism many of them give up on drawing altogether. As adults, they often feel distressed if asked to draw because their drawings resemble those of a ten year old. This is interesting as it pin points the arrested development of the right-brain.

Most people start a creative journey with their left-brain, which is a bit of a hindrance to say the least. The left-brain likes to name, number or categorize things in some way. These skills lend themselves to judgment, criticism and comparison – how helpful are they in our early creative endeavors! No wonder we give up so quickly.

Once we name things, we stop "seeing" them. Our left-brain has to process so much incoming information that it creates shortcuts (it thinks this is helpful.) When we look at objects, it quickly pulls up information from its internal filing cabinets like a hyper efficient secretary on steroids. It does this before we have a chance to really see them. Most of us are living in a left-brain virtual reality that has become so familiar; we can no longer distinguish it from reality itself.

If we want to be creative, we need to replace analysis with a willingness to play and make random, intuitive choices. On the other hand, we also need huge amounts of discipline. Now that the 'C' word is such a fabulous thing, we must ensure we don't swing to the other side of the pendulum. Some parents have given up disciplining their children for fear of restricting the inspiration, just as many schools give up on grammar and sentence construction in favor of creative writing.

Who knows what the workforce will look like in the next generation. With everyone raised on the bible of self-belief, and qualifications in media studies, it's going to be pretty difficult to find a plumber.

Having been raised in the dour north, I am equally guilty of wanting to bestow a magical, fun filled, creative life on my children. My daughter recently did work experience in a forensic laboratory. She had long been fascinated by the subject matter and was considering it as a career option. At the end of the week she realized what she actually wanted was to be the actress who plays the leading role in *Crime Scene Investigation*. Because this was so funny I agreed to send her to Performing Arts instead.

> Creativity demands freedom, but it also requires constraints. "Write a story about anything" is a hideously difficult exercise. "Write a story about a one armed private detective who arrives in a quaint English village in the winter of 1967" is much easier. The facts of the story may be meaningless and eventually discarded, but it's the discipline of creating within these confines that allows a greater meaning to surface. Discipline shapes our creativity.

It's all about balance. The right-brain loves to play in a safe playground. The left-brain creates the framework, the structure upon which the gleeful creative spirit can do somersaults, hang upside down and shout "Look Ma, no hands!"

The first dial on *the Sextant* should be one that determines the balance between left and right so that we can find "True North". This is an inner sense rather than a literal destination. If something feels true it has a "ring of truth" not a large signpost, or a mission statement of over enthusiastic words.

Meanwhile, the whirring sounds of an industrial chainsaw remind me of where I am now. Which direction would *the Sextant* point to?

Facts: We booked for a week but hadn't paid, as there was insufficient time to do a bank transfer. The cottage was available at short notice so we had not prevented it from being sold to anyone else.

The owner had been economical with the truth!

We packed our bags, left enough money for one night and ran away like Thelma and Louise.

And what's the meaning in the experience?

Pretending something is positive when it isn't can often be denial, delusion or self-sacrifice.

Martyrdom for a meaningless cause isn't "being nice" it's stupid.

Truth is a powerful thing... you shouldn't get economical with it.

Ever.

The lovely Chloe and the not so lovely recycling bins

DAY THREE

Word count on *The Sextant* has not reached the planned 4000 words! Only two days in and already behind schedule! Perhaps self-help isn't my genre. I'm beginning to wonder whether the decision to leave the world of fiction behind was the correct one. You can take the girl out of Romantic Comedy but you can't take... etc.

No. I am determined to be creative. I will write something serious and helpful for other people, so they can avoid the mistakes I made. My learning curve resembles the Milky Way in its scale and scope – complete with supernovas and black holes. Surely this can be put to some good use. I will leave the Romantic Comedy to Chloe - she's twenty years younger, falls in love with reckless abandon and is not concerned by the number of times her fingers get burnt. She's the perfect person to pass a flaming torch to.

In defense of my low word count, we did spend the whole of yesterday looking for somewhere else to stay, leaving no writing time whatsoever.

Self-Help Adage No. 3 Ask and it is given

I always find this one a bit hard to swallow. To the new agers, this is no big deal, you don't need to strive or work hard for anything, you just manifest the things you want. Whatever you ask for you can have. Just line yourself up to the frequency of whatever you desire and the Law of Attraction will bring it to you.

To the hard-core religious people, the above is a childish, indulgent misuse of a spiritual principle. You don't ask for things, you pray, and because God is all good and cares for his people he will answer your prayers. However there are caveats. Some religions frown on praying for material things like fast cars; or vanity things like thin thighs. Other religions are more flexible and you can ask for virgins and the slow and painful death of your enemies. Mostly religious people are like Miss World contestants – they say they're praying for World Peace but really they're praying for a bunch of other stuff.

Given a modicum of intelligence and a thin grasp of evolutionary theory, it is pretty absurd to imagine that God is nothing more than a big person (i.e. a much grander version of ourselves) however this is the view of most fundamentalist religions. For example if we're capable of loving (obviously just friends and family, let's not get carried away) God is ALL loving (and can even love his enemies). If we're capable of being angry, God can be *extremely* wrathful and create tsunamis, AIDS epidemics and death of the first-born.

The New Agers think this is all religious propaganda to keep people fearful, guilty and easy to control. (Actually a brilliant strategy that worked well for thousands of years, so well done the early Romans). New Agers think that God is Love with a capital L - the energy of love that drives the universe. Being energy, God doesn't have a gender or a body of any description, which is how he/she can be everywhere simultaneously, a bit like the genie in Aladdin's lamp only more liberal with the wishes. New Agers think that our thoughts create our reality.

I kind of prefer this version but there is a hitch! Praying - what is it exactly?

A prayer is a thought form with a clear intention.

Hmmm. Problem. Let's face it, most of our thoughts are a bit meandering. They start, a different thought interrupts them, and then they go off in another direction. We're generally not very good at focusing them. If the universe acts as a mirror, matching our thought forms and delivering on their requests, this makes for a lot of chaos – noticed any chaos in the universe lately?

There is a popular phrase "be careful what you wish for" meaning you really need to think about the end result of what you pray for otherwise you could end up with a different set of problems. A more up to date version of this phrase is "be careful what you think about." If God is energy, not form, then there is no difference between a thought and a prayer. In fact a prayer is a thought with a different name.

So it's not surprising that we've inadvertently created quite a lot of unwanted things in the world. As manifestors, we're all over the place with our random co-creations. However when something bad happens, we suddenly get a bit more clarity. "Please God don't let me have a parking ticket. I meant to leave the shop on time but then I saw the brown suede boots. Please... please... please." Note - lots of focus.

This counts as a prayer.

When you get back to the car and there's a ticket on the windscreen you can think one of three things:

1. God is angry with me for coveting the brown boots.
2. God doesn't exist - the world is random.
3. My vibration is not in alignment! I'm giving off the negative energy of "I'm scared I'm going to get a ticket." I should have been thinking happy thoughts like "Thank you angels for looking after my car (insert visualization of car with no ticket on) and giving the lovely parking attendant something else to focus on while I was in the shop."

Number three would be a good choice but there is a flaw in this manifesting business. Thoughts. On a good day just how many of our thoughts are conscious? How much of our brain do we use? Most scientific studies say about 5%. So if 5% of our thoughts are super positive conscious ones and 95% of our thoughts are – "who the hell knows" unconscious ones, how successful is our manifesting going to be?

Note to self. *The sextant* has to include a dial (possibly with annoying ring tone) for waking up parts of the unconscious mind so that we can find out what they're thinking about.

Back to France. We have now driven for four hours in search of a cottage or apartment that we can both write in. We are not asking for much. It has to be clean, warm and lovely. It has to have spectacular views. It has to be near a town where Chloe can smile at French boys with a view to kissing any exceptionally cute ones. It has to be near a restaurant where we can eat without having to cook, and close to a small shop where we can buy an extra bottle of wine at short notice when the muse has deserted us.

We stop at a small town for coffee and a local map and realize we are quite near the Pyrenees. Judging by how far we've come, it only looks another half hour drive. Two hours later we arrive. The road is steep, narrow and snakes around the mountains. The little car struggles with endless hairpin bends and inadequate gears, but the scenery is spectacular (first box on the list ticked) as we head into a deserted ski village.

All around us are pretty chalets. We find a tourist office where two bemused women tell us the season does not start for another two months and that most of the chalets are privately owned and let by the proprietor. They direct us to a lettings agency and we spend the next hour huddled over a computer screen going through line after line of chalets that are either too large, too small, too low down or don't have keys. The helpful lettings agent keeps shaking her head as we get to the end of yet another Excel spreadsheet. Suddenly her eyes light up as she discovers one last possibility. Her fingers fly across the keyboard opening and closing windows. Chloe and I are both praying at this point (lots of focus). There are keys! It's high up! It's the right size!

We get back in the little car and drive further up the mountain. The chalet is perfect. Chloe wanders through the rooms like Goldilocks and pronounces it "just right." Manifestation complete. We crawl into bed and hope our unconscious mind doesn't dream of three bears.

The proprietor of our perfect chalet

DAY FOUR

Self-Help Adage No. 4 Go with the Flow

I am going to start by writing my way through writer's block. All the books on creativity recommend stream of consciousness writing. The idea is that our mind is full of random thoughts, reruns of scenes from the past, fantasies of scenes from the future, conversations we wish we'd had and some we hope to have, lists of stuff we need to remember and excerpts from popular songs (how annoying are these?).

In the midst of all this noise, the very quiet creative voice is trying to be heard. It would be nice to think that with practice this voice could develop a decent set of lungs and be a bit more vocal, but sadly we are now in the realm of energy not form. The only way to hear the creative voice is to turn down the volume on all that other noise.

Stream of consciousness writing aims to get all the random thoughts down on the page (and therefore out of our head), which frees up more space. If we keep going as fast as possible this works – suddenly, out of the mish mash of trivia, a new original thought appears. Of course if we write too slowly, it gives our brain enough time to pull up endless amounts of unlovely, inconsequential stuff... so we could write all day and produce nothing remotely publishable. Unless of course we're considering a career with *Hello* magazine.

Another way to receive inspiration is to ask ourselves penetrating questions. Or, as they say in the world of strategy "If you want a better answer, ask a better question." OK here goes.

Q: What is creativity?

Ha! In the old days this was easy to answer. It's all about art with a capital A - in other words painting, writing and music. Children were assessed after primary school and the creative ones chose Art, and the non-creative ones chose Science, and "never the twain shall meet." Of course now that we live in the age of energy we have a much broader definition. Creativity is the energy with which we do anything, so we can have creative scientists or creative electricians.

We were all tuned in to this source of inspiration once, but most of us lost our connection early on. If creative expression is not endorsed (in all its many forms) then children start to close it down and instead they learn to memorize facts. The up side of facts is that they are never wrong. And even if they are found to be incorrect, we didn't invent them, somebody else did; we just had to learn them, so either way we're in the clear.

If we have a fear of humiliation or a fear of failure (welcome to the human race) there are many advantages to the facts and logic of the left-brain. Sadly, in our rush to embrace them, many babies were thrown out with much bath water. Who knows how many creative dreams were dashed or sucked down plugholes in our attempts to learn the rules? Note: this does not constitute "being in the flow."

However, the universe doesn't like the static rigidity of facts. It likes creation. It likes to witness form emerging from the chaos. It's no fun watching random images of chaos and possibility, when we could be watching an incredible movie with a beginning, a middle and an end; and hopefully some exciting car chases, comedy moments and great sex. It's almost our duty to deliver this, not just for ourselves but also for the rest of humanity. We're supposed to live bold, brave lives that touch other people, inspire them or make them laugh.

It could be said that creativity is the "Intel inside"' added value thing, that turns something good into something great. We can all write, draw or speak but many of us can't evoke a response of tears, laughter, joy or inspiration when we do so. Grace does this. Grace comes to meet us when we get into the flow. It's our creative partner. True creativity is co-creativity.

Of course we need to be humble and respectful and realize that though it is called "co-creativity" this is not a 50/50 deal. Our part is the smallest part – at least it is if we want to produce anything that's really good. If our ego gets involved, and we get carried away by the brilliance of our creations, the flow of ideas often dries up.

Before working in advertising I worked in rock and roll, which is an interesting landscape in which to observe the above dynamic. Like many people who are afraid of humiliation and therefore refuse to develop their own creativity, I became fascinated by the creativity in others, and liked to be near them. This is also known as vicarious living or "I like to be near the light, to see the light, but I don't like the light to see me!"

Note to self: *The Sextant* needs another dial to tease out hidden unconscious guilt - after all why would anyone not want a light to shine on them? What imagined crimes have we committed that we hide so compulsively from the spotlight? These are pretty big questions so we must be on the right track. We just need some heavyweight answers to begin their download into our consciousness.

Back to rock and roll. In the old days the trajectory of most musicians was one of:

- Emergence (from the original background they were rebelling against)

- Growth (development of musical talent)

- Peak (third album syndrome)

- Egocentricity (I'm so brilliant... It's all about Me)

- Demise (Oh dear I can't seem to write a tune that works - perhaps recreational drugs could help).

You could say this is the journey from emergence to emergency...

Artistes were deemed to peak on their third album. In creative self-help books, with their "stream of consciousness" theories, this would mean the first two albums were getting all that random stuff out of the head before the really good stuff could come through. Depending on the "alignment" and humility of the artist, this "winning streak" could last for one album (Terence Trent D'arby) or it could last for a lifetime (Bruce Springsteen aka God). Actually Eric Clapton, Bob Dylan, Al Green, John Lee Hooker etc are also up there. (I prefer the Greek system of many Gods.)

The rock and roll industry has changed beyond recognition and pubs up and down the country bear witness to tales of how great it was in the old days as ex roadies recount hilarious tales for the price of a pint. Artistes nowadays are often created overnight by business moguls rather than honed by the experience of life on the road. As fast as they are "made" they can be "unmade." There is often insufficient time to develop a relationship with the "co" in the "co-creativity."

Veterans of rock and roll have built a relationship with the muse over time and a relationship with their fellow travelers in less than ideal space. Many great relationships are forged when we overcome difficulties by uniting against imposed constraints. An easy, idle life doesn't bring out the best in us. The roadies of yesteryear may have complained about dreadful venues - humping black boxes up the narrow stairs of old theatres or attempting to rig lighting trusses from the low ceilings of nightclubs - but these hardships brought out an ingenuity in them that would not have emerged in purpose built arenas with state of the art facilities. The bands they looked after may not have liked the *Fawlty Towers* accommodation, the dressing rooms that resembled toilets or the smell of burning as the front truss singed their hair; but they wouldn't have missed it for the world. After all, it's hard to write a killer album in the Four Seasons Hotel.

So back to creativity, "Our natural state of Grace." If we had it as children and we don't have it now, we need to go on a journey, retrace our steps, and find out where we lost it. This journey that Chloe and I have embarked on may be literal (or literary) but it mirrors the inner journey to the center of a vortex, that place of alignment where it's possible to be in the flow.

Or in the immortal words of Pink Floyd... "Set controls for the heart of the sun."

Eve and the apple... or Eleanor and the Apple Mac. Plus ca change - though the tree of knowledge is looking a little sparse.

DAY FIVE

Self-Help Adage No. 5 **Perception is projection**

Our first proper day of writing (at least six hours!). Chapter One is complete but perhaps needs an illustration. Though *the Sextant* is a metaphysical tool, I have made a drawing of what it would look like in physical form. There are already lots of dials, the idea being that each day (or certainly before any major decisions) you could check your position, check your *perception* of your position, re-adjust and move forwards.

Perception is a key thing. As more of the unconscious realm becomes conscious, our perception of events and people begins to change - albeit sometimes slowly. We love the idea of instant transformation. This kind of perceptual change is a bit like the conversion of Saul on the road to Damascus...

"Christians terrible people... "

(Flash of lightning)

"Christians best people in the world!"

If there was a tool available for instant transformation, it would resemble a kaleidoscope rather than a sextant. We would look through a tube containing colored shapes and see one picture, then turn the cylinder a couple of degrees anticlockwise and see a whole new picture!

This is often called an "Epiphany" or "Enlightenment" and is a much sought after state in the creative world. However it can have its drawbacks. There are consequences to downloading that amount of light that fast, and some mystics (not to mention many LSD taking hippies) have become a little unstuck by the whole process. Building a solid foundation first is a good idea.

A human being has a mind, a body and a spirit. For the most part (certainly in the western world) our mind is our best friend. It's the one we spend most time with, so is the most developed of all three. The body and the spirit lag way behind. (Obviously vitamin popping gym fanatics with an antioxidant addiction or meditating yoga enthusiasts with a chanting disposition, this does not apply to you.)

We have a love-hate relationship with our mind. When our thoughts are good we're happy, when they're not we're miserable. We seem to have no control over our thoughts. Everything can be going along swimmingly, then something happens and "pow" - the mind turns the kaleidoscope 180 degrees and everything becomes dark and gloomy. The spirit could be saying "just turn it the other way!" but it's difficult to do this when your hands are in the ammunition jar and your body's sulking in the corner plotting revenge. We need to make the spirit and the body stronger if we are going to take on the superior strength of our mind.

Occasionally we get to the point where we've had enough of our inflexible friend – this usually happens on New Years Eve, when we declare, "things will be different from now on." We empty the fridge of bad things to eat, stock up on health food, join a gym and sign up for a half marathon. We want the "epiphany" for the body. A couple of weeks later we give up – our muscles ache and our body craves its addictions. The sensible thing would be to slowly build a solid framework for the new lifestyle to hang on. Muscle doesn't develop overnight. A new mantra doesn't make an addiction disappear.

As children we grew up with fairytales. Most of these didn't include actual fairies but this generic title implied the "other worldliness" of the story, which always involved a transformation of some sort by a magic wand or a spell. We love this instant transformation stuff, but it's kid's fantasy... and for good reason. After being knocked out by the light, Saul (now renamed Paul) was not the most balanced person in the world. The word "obsession" springs to mind. Mystics tread a thin line between brilliance and madness, as the surgeon who stitched up Van Gogh's ear will testify. We can't suddenly decide we want to "live in the flow" of the creative spirit without putting in some groundwork. We need to build spiritual muscle.

Note: next addition for *The Sextant* - a gauge to check balanced "mind-body-spirit" levels.

In the meantime Chloe and I, having actually completed a creative workout in the metaphysical realm, can return to the literal one. We leave the lofty heights of the mountain chalet and head down to the local town. Town implies lots of people, shops, restaurants, and general bustle, however this being an out of season ski resort, most of the town is closed for business. We drive around the near empty streets and realize there are only two places showing any signs of life. One is a casino, so we enter the second one, which appears to be a normal bar. Despite the fact that there are so few people, they seem to represent all aspects of the village. There's the traditional innkeeper, some local tradesmen, a few disaffected teenagers, the smallest man in the world... and Elvis.

This is so bizarre that we order wine and start taking photographs. What would be pretty normal in London (it would probably be difficult to go out for the evening and not meet someone dressed up as Elvis) is intriguing and magical. Nobody speaks a word of English so we struggle to summon up enough French vocabulary to comprehend the narrative of our fellow drinkers. As we get through a bottle of wine our understanding becomes greater and we are amazed at our sudden ability to communicate.

The casino now seems the obvious place to go. A solitary figure at the reception desk greets us. Night workers all seem to have the same haunted expression, or is it just the lighting that makes them appear so? The "casino" comprises a dozen slot machines and an empty black jack table. There is a bar running the entire length of one wall with a neat line of empty chairs. As our level of alcohol drops so does our ability to project wonderment on this sad scenario. We decide to head back to the chalet but Chloe notices one last neon light. We follow the star - she is on a quest to meet French boys.

Inside there is life! An animated group of old men sit in front of an assortment of bottles. We join the tableau and with our newly discovered mastery of French, delight the natives with descriptions of our lives to date. They want to know where we come from and what we do. "We are writers!" It sounds even more enchanting in French. "Nous sommes ecrivons!!" we declare to the universe with conviction. More alcohol is produced. It seems to be assumed that strong alcohol is the fuel of choice on the writer's journey.

They are full of questions now. Are we married? (I am divorced and Chloe is single) Shock all round as man with elaborate handlebar moustache inches forwards and orders champagne. The bar keep is joined by his lovely assistant, a young woman who arrives in motorbike leathers and Darth Vader helmet. Removing the helmet she greets everyone in the bar by kissing them on both cheeks. This takes some time. The door opens and in walks... Elvis, and the smallest man in the world! Chloe breathes a sigh of relief. At last somebody under the age of 40 that she can flirt with.

However after a very brief hello (involving no kisses) Elvis disappears to the other side of the bar to engage in a strange boy greeting ritual involving pushing, wrestling and arm/neck locks, leaving Chloe with his vertically challenged friend.

On the slow, very inebriated walk back to the chalet, we comment on the fact that this is not what we had in mind when we decided to embark on the spirit filled life.

Elvis and the smallest man in the world

DAY SIX

Wake up with a hangover after a sleepless night. Chloe had a dream in which she had emailed her ex boyfriend, only to discover on checking her blackberry that it hadn't been a dream after all.

Self-Help Adage No. 6 **If you love someone let them go**

If we have not been going to Spiritual Gym regularly, what we really mean is "let them go so they can come back" which is not the same thing at all. Our hidden agenda here is to undertake a magic wand style transformation by losing weight, restyling hair or buying new clothes while they are *temporarily* gone. When we *accidentally* run into them we will act cool and emotionally mature so that they become desperate for us to reconsider our decision.

The problem with the spirit is that it doesn't play by the rules of the mind. Mental strategies work on a sliding scale of results, but the spiritual laws of energy are more exact. If we are not 100% truthful, they don't work at all! That's why *the Sextant* is necessary - we're talking precision engineering here. One degree either side may not look like anything but when we're going at light speed, we can miss our destination by a million miles.

I am trying to write through the hangover but am consumed by thoughts of French bread and apricot jam, so have to stop to rush down to the Boulangerie. What is it with creativity? As soon as you embark on a creative journey "Obsession" becomes your new best friend. Chloe is sitting with her laptop but her eyes are fixed on her blackberry, which refuses to ping with any form of reply.

Letting go is about not getting attached to stuff. If we want to navigate our way through the world of energy, we need to remove our attachment to form. This is tricky, as form appears to have enormous magnets that pull us in. We set off with good intentions and pretty soon we are caught in the gravitational pull and end up going in circles around "Planet Addiction."

Addictions take many forms but they fall into two main categories:

> Mark 1: Addictions of the broken heart. These include food, alcohol, self-pity and romantic fiction.

> Mark 2: Addictions of the ego. These include work, money, cocaine and Bruce Willis movies.

Like many adolescents, when I was thirteen I fell in love with sadness. Anna Karenina, Ophelia, Madam Bovary and a bunch of Pre Raphaelites were my recreational drugs. Dark glamour is just so seductive (and of course the clothes are very flattering). I looked forward to developing a taste for absinthe while freezing in a Parisian apartment.

Once I left home and joined the world of rock and roll, I was horrified by this error of judgment, as I saw the modern equivalent of these women portrayed by country and western songs (how glamorous now?!) Lyrics along the lines of "If you leave me I'll die" were a sort of epiphany for me. I pitied people who had so little power and promptly swopped my addictions for the Mark 2 "Ego" variety. No more being the victim, let's kick ass and take names. What can I say? It's hard to exercise humility when you have a pocket full of backstage passes.

Of course in this world of duality, nothing is ever as it seems. I soon learned that far from being powerless, the Victim has a lot of power. Like a vampire they suck power from others while looking pale, interesting and innocent. We've all done it and then hidden the evidence by showing off our new cool addictions. As far as the creative spiritual life is concerned there's no difference between a good or bad addiction, it's all attachment to form so there are no winners here.

It's a bumpy ride along the road to creativity. We want to fly in the high clouds of inspiration but we also want to feel grounded and safe. We want the ideas to come quickly, but we're scared of speed. Instead of developing a different relationship to time and space we attempt a hotchpotch of a compromise. We form addictions so that we have an excuse to stay anchored to something. This keeps us from flying and slows down our progress.

Creativity is all around us, all the time, but we don't trust that it's there because we've existed on crumbs for so long. There is an interesting story of a poor boy who trespassed on the King's land to steal food. It was the King's birthday, and being benevolent he dismissed any charges and invited the boy to the celebratory banquet. During the feast the boy ate nothing, despite being offered plates full of food. At the end of the evening the Queen noticed the boy's hands. They were clenched tight holding onto the fragments of food he had stolen earlier in the day. He was unable to let go of what he had in order to have access to the abundance that was on offer.

This is what we do energetically every day. We need to un-prize our fingers and let go of our habitual addictions so that we can be open to receive new things.

Meanwhile Chloe is trying to figure out a double letting go strategy for her two ex boyfriends - one very recent (let's call him Simon Cowell because he works in rock and roll) and one she hasn't seen for 18 months (he's definitely more of a Captain Jack Sparrow). Jack Sparrow is the dark eyed ski instructor she once lived with in Switzerland. Every day here brings fresh reminders of their passionate high altitude romance. As we were driving through the Pyrenees, it was touch and go whether she would turn the wheel 90 degrees and head off for an entirely different mountain range.

Chloe is addicted to love. This is not the same as being addicted to sadness. It's more of an addiction to the *intensity* of being in love. I think the male equivalent is bungee jumping. There is an element of not being quite sure you'll survive the experience. In the main, adrenaline sports are a little less destructive than romance as you are only in a relationship with a piece of elastic which is fairly compliant with your wishes. Human beings, on the other hand, have all sorts of opposing desires – for example travel plans, glittering careers and other women – so the possibility of being crashed into the rocks of major heartbreak are quite high.

It's so difficult to get this right, as it seems we have to make an either or choice. Either be in a relationship that is safe, with someone who is not given to passionate desires (this means they won't leave) or be in a relationship with someone who adores you (but is equally likely to adore building a business empire, deep sea diving, and your best friend). The former is boring, the latter exciting but comes with a health warning. Is there no way we can navigate ourselves to a relationship in the heart of the paradox? Oh yes... *the Sextant*!

There needs to be another four dials on *the Sextant,* over which will sit four key characters or guardians with whom we have to negotiate to get our creative power back. This is definitely becoming a hero's journey! A Wizard of Oz style adventure in which we upgrade our mind, find our heart, develop our courage and thereby write some killer prose.

Good! We like riddles and challenges. Bring on the four guardians we have to do battle with. The first one is "the Victim." Our addictions point us towards this one. Now let's discover the identity and location of the other three!

Heaven in Planet Addiction

DAY SEVEN

Self-Help Adage No. 7 **I am an innocent man**

OK this is a Billy Joel song (as well as a self-help adage) but who better to take us into the whole arena of guilt. As we saw on Day 4 (I want to see the light, but I don't want the light to see me!) we need to become aware of our unconscious guilt. Creative energy won't show up if we continually hide our light under a bushel. This is where we encounter the challenge of the second guardian – the Child.

Christians say, "unless you become as little children you cannot enter the Kingdom of Heaven" – in other words unless you ditch the guilt and become innocent again you won't be receiving a laminate pass to enter the creative realm. So why can't we do this? We seem to be extremely reluctant to give up our guilt.

Jesus knew a thing or two about people. Knowing how much they loved guilt, he came up with a grand plan; he would elect to absorb all the guilt of humanity and sacrifice himself so that humanity might be free to start again with a clean slate. Of course like all best laid plans this went a bit awry. Now the Christians felt even more guilt! Far from feeling happy about being released from their imaginary prisons, they knelt before crucifixes feeling bad for centuries. Like all mystics, Jesus lived "in the now" so perhaps he couldn't predict our future obsession with dark glamour and suffering.

The love-hate relationship we have with guilt means that unless we have opted for "Mark 1 addictions" (heartbreak, donuts, country and western songs, and tequila) we hide it in our unconscious mind. That leaves everyone with "Mark 2 addictions" (work, status, pilates, popularity and expensive brands) wondering why nothing feels as great as it should. It's the unconscious guilt stupid! This is also the reason we sabotage our success. If we have guilt (wherever we've stashed it) we won't allow ourselves success. "We are not worthy."

This is a very sticky situation. To experience this in action, do the following exercise. First remember something you feel really bad about. Just pull it up in your mind. It could be something you did last week, or something you did in childhood. Lean into it, remember all the details, cringe, feel uncomfortable. Ask yourself how long you could hold on to that feeling. As Catholics will testify, the answer is a very, very long time. It's so sticky it's hard to get rid of.

Now do the opposite. Pull up in your mind a really happy time when you felt innocent, peaceful or joyful. Try holding on to this feeling. Most people crack after a few minutes. This is quite a good way to work out your innocence/guilt ratio. Clearly we have a bit of work to do on this.

Why are we so good at feeling bad! And now that we're adults how can we "become like little children." A lot of workshops and self-help books take this literally and put people in rooms with crayons and building bricks. HR departments develop initiatives involving "group hugs" or encourage people to "talk about their feelings." To normal people, this often feels artificial and contrived. If people are put outside their natural comfort zone they will pretend. It's what we do. We know how to act nice when people are annoying and we know how to fake bonding when the situation requires. We do it long enough to get to the end of the session and then we breathe a sigh of relief.

Let's retrace our steps and discover where we lost our natural (not fake) innocence so that we can reclaim it. For most of us this is back in childhood. We now enter the world of psychotherapy pioneered by Sigmund Freud and Carl Jung. They were both brilliant people, however they also underestimated the lure of dark glamour and our love affair with guilt. As fast as they "healed" one pattern, another one emerged to take its place. Nature documentaries give us many examples of primitive creatures that have the capacity to grow back missing parts of their anatomy. This is what we do with the wounds in our mind. This is why psychotherapy didn't work – our "Victim" is too unconscious.

We were all wounded as children. Growth usually causes pain. None of us were treasured enough, praised enough or loved enough according to the unrealistic expectations we had of other human beings. Many of us have a vague sense of feeling orphaned in the universe or a real sense of not belonging in our family of origin. This is a given - if we're perceiving through the mind. Now that we know our mind is not our best friend let's look through a different lens...

Imagine being part of a vast source of energy, curious about having a physical experience. In order to do this we need to get a body. We descend into the world of form via two people who become our parents and look after us until our five senses develop. We then forget all about our true ancestry (the energy of endless possibility) and look around at a world that we can't quite comprehend.

By the time we learn to communicate, it's too late! We've been assimilated into a world of scarcity, problems and pain. Our kaleidoscope is welded firmly in place and the picture isn't a pretty one. But *the Sextant* trumps the kaleidoscope. It has more dials! We don't have to settle for this conspiracy, we just have to remember who we are! The reason for the popularity of Harry Potter is just that. Children (and adults) are instinctively drawn to the archetypal figure of the magical child who can change reality.

So, the second of the four guardians with whom we have to negotiate to get our power back is the Child. The child will always be with us because it's an essential part of our spirit. It allows us to play with the energy. But in order to play creatively we have to transform the wounded child into a magical one, turn the guilty child into an innocent one and the orphaned child into a divine one. Otherwise our creativity will be labored, artificial or destructive.

Meanwhile in the mountains of France, Chloe is still battling with the Victim. In her quest to feel more victorious, she decides on the bold move of deleting "Simon Cowell" from her blackberry. As his number disappears from the address book, he is no longer "temporarily gone." Unless he contacts her there will be no way to reach him. She also deletes all his email and text messages, the ones she re-reads on occasion, to remind herself of the time when all his passion was directed towards her. The empty screen is shocking and slightly frightening.

I can't think of any words of advice or consolation. I remember my own experience of letting go. It was bewildering and unreal to be uncoupled from my husband. Friends, shocked by my rapid descent towards the rocks, were quick to point out the positive aspects of freedom. I could catch the wind like an eagle and fly! Or, if I was reluctant to soar and unsure of the destination, I could float like a butterfly on the breeze, smelling the flowers on the way!

My perception at that time was somewhat different. I had no sextant, and my floating experience more closely resembled that of an astronaut whose lifeline had been cut. I could only experience darkness while waiting for a slow airless death where no-one could hear me scream. Ground control to Major Tom...

I don't want to trivialize Chloe's feelings with a self-help aphorism so suggest we go for a long walk. It is freezing cold and sunny. The silence feels intense as if the air is newly pregnant. As we become accustomed to the lack of noise, we start to hear the faint sounds of distant cowbells, and the occasional gurgling of a stream. The path we walk is stony and unyielding. Yet, miraculously, peeping out of the hard ground are these incredible purple flowers. They have every reason under the sun to hide; yet they completely defy the limitations placed on them by terrain and climate.

They haven't forgotten who they are.

We can learn much from them.

Some seeds fall on stony ground, yet miraculously they still manage to grow up... into perfect flowers.

DAY EIGHT

Simon Cowell emails! Nothing major, just a short message sending Chloe greetings from some backstage bar, but it is a sign! The law of attraction works! If we let go of our addictions and attach our umbilical cords to the universal mother ship, we are rewarded. What other addictions can we uncouple ourselves from? I look at the bread and apricot jam but consider this a bridge too far. I haven't built enough spiritual muscle yet to give up sugar. I am still doing snowploughs on the nursery slopes of my highest potential. A morning walk to consider the dynamics of manifestation will do for now.

Self-help adage No. 8 Get out of your own way

Being cynical (though I prefer to call it realistic) I cannot quite believe the visualization thing. All those testimonials from self-help writers who got exactly what they wanted by cutting out pictures from magazines and making collages. My left-brain wants to know the statistics – how many people has this worked for and how many has it failed? What distinguishes the winners from the losers?

I understand the visual thing is important because images are more powerful than words. I saw this first hand in the advertising industry. A strong image stays in the mind longer than a well written strap-line. When we review history we do so pictorially. We don't remember the date the US pulled out of Vietnam but we remember the crying, naked children running from the napalm.

A picture engages the right-brain and we need access to the right-brain in order to recover our lost creativity. A graphic representation of our future vision is therefore a very good idea. We know how muddled, confused and unconscious most of our thoughts are. Once we can "see" what we want, the universe can respond better. A picture is something everyone can agree on, whereas a talked about idea can be interpreted in all sorts of different ways. How many times have we heard the phrase "Oh, but I thought you meant..."

So far so good, but what happens next in the visualization thing? According to the law of magnetic attraction, the new vision starts to make the journey from the world of energy to the world of form - it starts to manifest. In order to do this it has to come through us. We are the arms and legs, the eyes and ears of the creative energy. We build the buildings, create the art, and invent the technology. We are the vehicle through which creativity becomes manifest.

To this end, it would be prudent to look at what type of vehicle we are, what type of fuel we are running on and when was the last time we tuned the engine...

Getting ready for warp speed

The exciting part of Star Trek was always the bit where Scottie shouted frantically that they were going too fast and the shields wouldn't hold! The high tech Starship Enterprise suddenly seemed frail and vulnerable in the midst of a meteorite storm. It follows, that if we're about to embark on the journey of manifesting our highest creative potential, it would be prudent to check our vehicle and the circumstances in which parts of the ship might start falling off.

Here goes...

Vehicle health check...

Our physical body has seven energy centers or chakras. These centers are linked to the universe, via seven umbilical cords, through which information can go forward and back. Creative inspiration comes through a channel of energy to the top of our head. It then has to make its way down, through each of the energy centers, before it becomes physical form in the world. In the case of the mystics, this can happen very quickly as there's no gunk in the system stopping the energy flow. For most of the rest of us this happens either very slowly or not at all – the flow of inspiration gets blocked and the energy stays stuck somewhere in the body.

Not only does this make manifesting impossible, it is also bad news for the body, which is not designed to hold the energy of our unexpressed desires. The body creates little pockets, like nuclear silos, in which to store this energy. This is not ideal. We know the silos are there so we have to guard them carefully. We worry about radiation poisoning, which we attempt to ward off with detox diets and positive thinking. Sometimes, despite our best efforts, something can activate the stored energy leading to an explosion with Chernobyl like after effects.

We're going to run through these seven energy centers, like 007 – in other words, find the silos, release the hostages and blow up the bad guys. But first, an overview of the terrain. The following is the sequence by which an idea becomes reality through the seven chakras.

Seven: Crown of the head. No problems here, just lots of inspiration. The word "inspiration" comes from the Latin "in spirit" meaning the ideas are still in spirit form. Nothing can harm them. Nothing can kill them. This is the realm Jesus called "The Kingdom" as in "Seek first the Kingdom." This is the place to go to for good ideas (and eternal life).

Six: Just above and between the eyebrows. Here the idea comes into contact with the mind. This is where we think about the ideas and decide whether they are worth taking action on. Inspiration leaves the cosmos and enters the world of duality – is it a good or a bad idea? (Entirely subjective and the universe cares not a jot).

Five: The throat. Here, we language the idea. We start to talk about it. We discuss and make choices. This is where we are able to exercise the gift of free will bestowed upon us as conscious beings (animals don't have this – they're not given to conscious choices... or speaking in general).

Four: The heart. This is the bridge, the crossroads, the interface between thought and form. This is where we get the energy to make the idea happen. Do we love the idea? The universal energy of the cosmos is love, so the cord that connects us to this has a powerful force running through it. If we have ever felt heartbroken (that's most of us on the planet) we will have asked Scottie for the shields by now. This makes us feel safe but cuts us off from the energy supply. From now on we're running on reserve tank and consequently we start to drive very, very slowly for the rest of the descent.

Three: The solar plexus. Martial arts experts call this the center of our physical power. This is all about our "self identity". If we are strong in this area, nobody can push us over. Warriors practice deep breathing and pulling their focus from their head to this part of the body. If we have ever felt humiliated, if our sense of honor has ever been compromised (again most of us on this planet) we will have constructed concrete silos around these experiences. This slows down the energy no end. Many ideas whither and die in these silos.

Two: Sexuality. This is a very big deal. We know how powerful creative energy can be when it is expressed through our sexuality. We are now fully in the world of form (having lost contact with our identity as spirit) and we imagine that we need to control and direct this energy all by ourselves. This has some disastrous consequences. Most world religions try to control and repress sexual energy through the widespread dissemination of guilt. No wonder there are so many silos here, along with tombstones over our aborted creative projects. The "ideas" just didn't make it.

One: Birth. You only have to look above to see why so few inspirations actually make it into the physical world.

But all this can change! Just as James Bond had "Q" to equip him with state of the art gadgets, we just need to get out of our own way and ask for help.

I have to leave this journal for today, as I'm more determined than ever to build a tool for *the Sextant*! I keep doodling Da Vinci style drawings of ancient machinery with a modern twist and wonder if this counts as visualization. I might even cut them out and make a collage if I can find something sticky with which to attach them... now where's all that guilt when you need it?

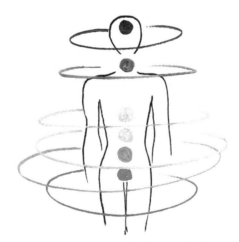

Chakra Khan - it's all about balance
(The tiger blood of Shere and the feminine funk of Chaka)

DAY NINE

Confidence: From the Latin *con fidare*, meaning "with faith."

Intoxicated by her newfound faith in the universe, Chloe is now going for the big one. It is time for her to let go of Jack Sparrow – her first love. This may not seem a big deal, but to anyone currently engaged in a similar procedure, they know different. The words "just let go" are not helpful; as they don't come anywhere close to expressing the enormity of what has to happen internally.

In order to elicit compassion for the addict and stimulation for the right-brain, I can offer the following image. (I heard this story so don't remember names, and can't even tell you if it's true - however it feels true, so none of this matters).

There was once a great tightrope walker. After years in the circus he wanted to challenge himself by walking the high wire across two tower blocks in the city. Because of the obvious danger, his aides came up with the idea of having an additional wire rigged, six feet below the original, so that he could grab onto this, if by chance he slipped. All his life he had walked a tightrope holding a balancing pole, and this day he stepped forward as usual. Half way across a gust of wind unsteadied him and he lost his balance. He must have seen the secondary wire but his hands were fixed firmly to the balancing pole and his mind was unable to let go of such a familiar object in order to grasp the new crutch that could have saved his life.

This is how hard it is for us to let go. As we plummet to our death, we know what makes sense, but habit and familiarity always over rule wisdom.

Self-help adage No. 9 **"If it hurts it isn't love."**
(Chuck Spezzano)

After "What is creativity?" here comes another big question...

Q: What is love?

We know love is a powerful energy that links to the heart. It allows us to be passionate activists for the things we care about. Without it, the human race would have died out a long time ago. Unless we create more of it, this could still become our reality. The love between a parent and a child ensures the child's survival and expands the capacity of the adult to feel. True love therefore benefits both the giver and receiver in equal measure.

But what about romantic love? This is trickier. We want to believe that it is unconditional and "for ever." We enter marriages on this basis. We fail spectacularly because of our addictions. Remember all those silos around our sexuality? Guess what's inside them...

Neediness.

If we haven't cured our addictions, love is always neediness. At the beginning, love is getting our needs met (hurrah!) At the end, love is not getting our needs met (boo!)

If we are taken over by our Victim, love is wistful and sulky - "If you really loved me you'd hack your way through this dense forest, defeat the guard, climb the tower and rescue me."

If we are taken over by our Child love is demanding - "If you really loved me you'd know what I want without me having to ask. You'd take care of me, make me feel safe and keep me entertained.

Remember there are four guardians with whom we have to meet and negotiate with, in order to win back our creative power. It's time to visit number three – the Prostitute.

Though we're talking about relationships, the Prostitute is not a literal one. It signifies our ability to negotiate our creative, financial or sexual power. We can be a prostitute at work (doing a job we hate, doing it badly, bitching about the boss, then taking the pay check). We can be a prostitute in a marriage (ditto all the above). We can prostitute our opinions (keeping quiet in order to be popular) and our conscience (I know it's wrong but my survival is under threat so I'll go along with it). Examples of the prostitute are endless.

We have all negotiated our power either through:
- Fear (if we're too scared to stand on our own feet)

- Laziness (if we just want to take the easy route)
- Need (if they've got something we want)

So back to Chloe's dilemma – her addiction to romantic love. For romantic love, we can now read "I will surrender my power if you deliver the things on my list." If a girl is raised on romantic fiction this list often involves the need for an alpha male. Alpha Male is the epitome of distant arrogant masculinity onto which we can project things like "silent strength" and "deep passion." Jack Sparrow had these traits in spades, so what went wrong?

The universe doesn't respond well when we negotiate our creative power. We're supposed to use it to fulfill our own unique purpose in life. When we give it away, bad things start to happen. This is a tough lesson, particularly for women. See who has the power in these popular stereotypes.

Boss/Secretary

Dad/Daddy's little Princess (fathers - please don't do this)

Knight/Damsel (this is very compelling until you play it through to its logical conclusion)

Knight/Damsel - the sequel. After the romantic rescue scene, the Knight leaves. His job is to fight battles, engage in quests and rescue other damsels - that's what Knights do. Damsels experience the high voltage drama of the rescue, followed by an awful lot of waiting around for the Knight's return. This gets boring, unless they become pre Raphaelites and turn yearning into an art form. Sometimes the Damsel feels compelled to get into more trouble - that's what Damsels do - necessitating rescue by another Knight, at which point the whole thing gets really messy.

We fall in love with the hero because we don't want to become the hero in our own story. But becoming the hero is our destiny and we are not allowed to refuse it. So time for some self-reflection, and a few exercises from the Grand Doyenne of the archetypal world, Caroline Myss.

Confronting the Prostitute

What type of person do you give your power away to? Do you lose your self-esteem around alpha males? How about intellectuals, artists, celebrities, rich people? Do you act differently around them?

Whose approval do you seek? Who is the person that would leave you feeling gutted if they stopped liking/loving/respecting you?

If we don't approve of ourselves, we try to get approval from others. This never works. They're under universal orders not to approve of us, so that we might get a grip, begin to like ourselves more and get on with our creative purpose.

Relationship dynamics are a bit like playing tennis with energy. I win today - you win tomorrow. Either way we get an excuse to avoid moving forward with our life. In an equal relationship both parties would encourage their partner's journey of creative expansion – even if that expansion threatened their own security. Instead of thinking "You need to stop doing that" they would think, "I need to make myself feel more secure."

This is premier league, but it's time to stop selling off our highest potential. Time to stop being pulled into the gravitational field of another person (no matter how fabulous) and going around in circles.

Meanwhile Chloe has sent a message to Jack Sparrow suggesting that, it would be good to talk. She's ready to heal the past and let it go. She has the confidence now... she just needs to dig deep for the courage to walk the tightrope empty handed, trusting that her true partner is at the other side, waiting to meet her.

Or in the words of the immortal Leonard Cohen.

> *Like a bird on a wire*
> *Like a drunk in a midnight choir*
> *I have tried, in my way,*
> *To be free*

Balance – don't try this at home

DAY TEN

Aarrgghhh!!! I cannot write. Work on *the Sextant* came to a grinding halt yesterday when I found I couldn't construct a single sentence that I was happy with. Flow ceased only to be replaced by inner angst. I tried going for a long walk but this just gave more space for the unhelpful voice in my head to keep up a constant one-way dialogue of unhelpful opinion.

You're kidding yourself - you can't write. You're a hypocrite - you can't even put into practice what you write about. (This part is true – I myself am still doing planetary orbits around an alpha male – more on him later!) *The Sextant won't work. You'll be revealed as a fraud, selling ineffective remedies from the back of a covered wagon.* The inner voices just won't stop.

This is what it must feel like to be mad. Walking along the stony path strewn with purple flowers, I am filled with compassion for the strange women who wander around London muttering incomprehensibly or talking loudly to invisible people. How can the inside of my head be this gloomy when I am surrounded by beauty and tranquility? The sky is blue and so clear that the mountains look as if someone has traced their outline with a sharp pencil. I feel as if I am in the idyllic pastoral landscape of a Disney cartoon. I expect squirrels to start up a conversation while over excited birds drop flower petals along the path ahead.

Mad indeed. Perhaps I need the familiar noise and bustle of city life, in order to appear calm and serene. By making my external reality so peaceful it seems I have inadvertently revealed the noise and chaos within. I feel like screaming or chloroforming the voices entirely. It being too early in the day to open a bottle of wine without embarrassment, I decide to drive to the nearest Boulangerie to buy the sweetest cake I can find. I practice my French phrases (*un gateaux grande avec beaucoup de sucre*) on my way back to the chalet, where I find Chloe in a state of mental torment. At last some displacement activity I can engage in. The relief of having an excuse to become involved in the drama of someone else's life is palpable.

Jack Sparrow has not replied. Chloe has re-read the email she sent him dozens of times but it reveals no craziness; just a breezy note informing him that, as she is currently in France, it might be a good idea to meet up. She didn't even add the lines "in order to get closure on the relationship so we can both move on."

I didn't venture the information that Jack Sparrow seems to have already moved on quite successfully (he is in fact living with another woman). Chloe, however, is convinced that he has not processed any of the feelings and is therefore "in denial." Meanwhile she has made up for his lack of accountability by revisiting their relationship on a regular basis for the past year and a half.

I did point out that one of the traits of the alpha male hero is that they are not given to very much self-reflection. This is not a criticism, just an obvious side effect of the lifestyle of that particular archetype. When the relationships of alpha males end, they tend to be single for about ten minutes before the next object of their affections comes along. In truth, other women have radar for the early warning signals of failed romance, so start gathering and preening even before the final closing of the door.

This (often dramatic) door slamming often has a sub text for women - in Chloe's case it went something like "the force of this door slam shows how much I am hurting which is your cue to run after me and reassure me how much I am loved." Unfortunately the sub text for men is more along the lines of "Clearly the door isn't the only thing in this room that's unhinged." This gives the perfect opportunity for the understudies in the wings, whose opening line is usually something along the lines of...

"She obviously didn't understand you, and is clearly crazy... I on the other hand... "

Why would Jack Sparrow not want to reply to Chloe's simple suggestion?

The question "Can we talk?" strikes fear into the heart of every man, and is normally interpreted as "Can I tell you where you went wrong." But Chloe's intention was pure. She just wants closure. I want a reasonable word count. I suspect Jack wants sex without any complicated emotions.

Chloe hacks off slices of bread and covers them in apricot jam. She tries to imagine what is going through Jack's head. *Perhaps he still loves her and is afraid of what he might feel, should he see her again. This is a much bigger problem. What if they both move forward, marry other people (the wrong people!), then meet one day on the ski slopes? Disaster! And now there are children involved! But it's their destiny to be together. The heartbreak is magnified a hundredfold. Surely he has to see the logic in this.*

Suddenly my madness is brought into context and I don't feel so crazy anymore. There are not many advantages of age (in our youth obsessed society) but this is one of them. I suggest a trip to the supermarket. Chloe stares at her blackberry like a forlorn French princess observing the guillotine. This small black device could save or end her life. I feel maternal, in a Marie Antoinette kind of way and suggest it's probably a good time to eat cake.

Self-help adage No. 10 Leadership requires humility and an iron will

So now that we have talked about the victim, the child and the prostitute, there's one remaining guardian with whom we need to negotiate. This is the Saboteur. When we've fought the good fight and the prize is so near we can almost touch it, this is the smiling figure that blocks the path. The Saboteur is a tricky character. It is smart and cunning. We think we know what it looks and sounds like – a hooded villain full of negative pronouncements. In fact it is way more subtle than this...

It is all the voices in our head.

If we decide to go on a journey to find our lost creativity, far from ridiculing us, the saboteur will say something like "How fascinating... that's somewhere I've always wanted to go... I can help you". Like the Iago character in *Othello*, the Saboteur will pretend to be our new best friend, agreeing enthusiastically with everything we want to do, then throwing in seeds of doubt before innocently walking away.

It is only when those seeds of doubt have sprouted into bushes, obscuring our path, that the Saboteur says "Come on, you tried, perhaps it's not meant to be. We can stop here, the view is lovely; let's build a campfire and open a bottle of wine."

This is when we have to really step up to the plate. The only way we can defeat the saboteur is to develop leadership qualities. In the old days, leadership was all about pride, arrogance and telling everyone else what to do. Now that we understand energy a little more, we know how ineffective this is. Commanding others to do things, whether by fear or by dangling carrots, is not a successful strategy. We may perform the task but we do so with bad grace, which tends to make for a sub standard outcome.

Commanding ourselves to do things is equally futile. If we are not in full alignment with the request, we find all sorts of ways to resist its execution. This is particularly true of any creative challenge. We have to lead ourselves out of our current malaise by developing self-respect and embracing seemingly paradoxical qualities – the blending of humility with an iron will.

The journey we are on is co-creative. The universe provides the inspiration. Our part in the "co" is to keep the faith and struggle on regardless of obstacles (*this is the iron will part*). After we have achieved greatness we need the humility to understand that it was not all about us - we were helped (*this is the humility part*).

The Saboteur is skilled at creating obstacles. Rather than fighting the obstacle or wrestling with the Saboteur, it helps if we accept and work alongside them. The Saboteur is part of our mind so we are in effect just fighting ourselves, which is a waste of energy. Alignment is all about becoming part of the same team. In any team, there are always members who grumble, ridicule or sulk in corners. We just need to bring them all back into the center.

The phrase "being centered" usually implies an easy place we get to after a few deep breaths and some peaceful thoughts. Not so - sometimes it is more like struggling with the G force while driving the Millennium Falcon through a meteorite storm. Everything in the universe conspires to pull us out.

This is an illusion of course. The universe is friendly and the conspiracy is entirely within ourselves. Our mind creates all the drama, because it doesn't want our creative spirit to emerge. After playing such an important role for so long, it hates the idea of becoming redundant or marginalized to the cheap seats. *Don't you know who I am?* The mind is determined to prove it is "who we are." Our spirit, having been bound and gagged and hidden in a basement for all these years has some catching up to do.

Time to take out a membership to spiritual gym. The spirit is an intangible thing, and on the whole, we don't deal very well with intangibles. Our best course of action against the tyranny of the mind is for our spirit to form an alliance with the body. When the spirit and the body team up against the mind they have a stronger chance of leveling the playing field.

We need Caroline's wisdom again.

Confronting the Saboteur

Pick one physical goal (any goal will do) and make a commitment to it. Consistency is the key here (not grandiosity of the goal).

Some examples: walk 20 minutes every day, do the washing up without sighing (even though it's not your turn); smile at every person that serves you (even the ones who don't make eye contact); limit your Internet surfing to one hour a day (or television/video games/Facebook); give something away every week (shoes, clothing, money); Do something significant for another person once a month (clean out their garage, look after their kids).

The task is not significant; it's the consistency that's important. It sends a signal from the body to the spirit. The signal says, "I'm a force to be reckoned with. I won't abandon you like some fair-weather friend as soon as the Saboteur comes calling, regardless of what cool plans he has for the evening."

It takes discipline to develop the iron will necessary to stay positive in a negative world, particularly when complaining and resentment are such popular default settings, but the results speak for themselves. "Those who say it can't be done shouldn't get in the way of people who are already doing it."

I have been lucky enough to witness some incredible examples of iron will in action. My own teacher Caroline Myss lectures all over the world and writes prolifically. She doesn't complain about the difficulty of fitting all this in. She just sleeps less. Her body and spirit have cut some kind of deal to allow this to happen. She doesn't even keep photographs. She's got so much to do in this "now" moment that she has no desire to indulge in nostalgia. Obviously most of us can't match this level of discipline, (Caroline is pretty hard core) but we can all do better than we are doing currently.

Meanwhile back in France, I am sitting in a small café with Chloe, eating pain au chocolat, curious about the fact that wheat intolerance seems to have bypassed the French nation.

Though I can't understand the commentary, my eyes are drawn to the television screen in the corner showing rolling news coverage of a leader with humility and an iron will. In a film clip no longer than two minutes I watch Barack Obama addressing huge crowds of people, getting on and off planes to shake hands with foreign dignitaries prior to long meetings. I know that when he emerges, he will still face the daily work of creating new visions for an ailing health service, and a complex financial one before putting his kids to bed and spending time with his wife.

Context is everything. In the light of all this, surely I can write one freaking book!

Waiting for the blackberry that doesn't ping

DAY ELEVEN

Success! I am back on track. Yesterday saw the emergence of new dials on *The Sextant* and some idea of the premise for the book. It is a clarion call to the unconventional and the rebellious; a toolkit for harnessing and directing creative energy; the "kiss of life" for an ailing society.

In the bible, there is a fitting metaphor used to describe the beginning of humanity. God took the dust and "breathed life into it." If we are going to reach our next level of evolution as conscious creators, we must breathe life into our creations.

In the fairy tales, powerful spells can only be broken by "the kiss of true love." Not only do we have to breathe life into our intentions - we have to love and honor them!

If we are going to visit the realm of higher consciousness (after all, that's where the creativity comes from) symbolism and metaphors help us communicate there. Words alone are a bit inadequate. Images and stories help to bridge the gap between the physical and the spiritual. I can describe a physical journey and everyone will have the same frame of reference – we can "see" both the traveller and the scenery. But a journey to reclaim the creative spirit within? What is the spirit? Is it the same thing as a soul? Is it "who we really are?"

Self-help adage No. 11 Know Thyself

Spiritual concepts are a bit like philosophical ones and I used to struggle with these as well. One of the most famous French philosophers was Rene Descartes. He came up with the often-quoted phrase, "I think therefore I am." In other words because I can think - I exist. This implies that "who we are" is the part of us that thinks. In other words, we could remove bits of our body but as long as we have a brain that thinks, we can still experience consciousness.

This has led to some pretty wacky concepts like cryogenics, whereby people have their head frozen after death so that in the future, when scientists figure out how to live forever, they can have their brain put into something else and thereby continue their experience of consciousness. The phrase "more money than sense" springs to mind.

There is a part of us that is eternal. It is the part that experiences consciousness... but it isn't in the brain.

Some time after Rene, another French philosopher Jean Paul Sartre refuted Rene's concept and came up with another gem. "The consciousness that says 'I am' is not the consciousness that thinks." In other words we are not our thoughts. Similarly we are not our emotions. We are the awareness that sits behind the thoughts and emotions.

It took me ages to get this one, because like most people, I have to spend a lot of time using my left-brain. My enlightened friend John Marshall, who has more patience than I can comprehend, used to coach me through dark emotions with the question "The part of you that's noticing how sad you are... is she sad?" In other words, as Jean Paul realized, if you can observe the fact that you're having a thought or a feeling, another aspect of consciousness has shown up. Which part is this?

Our language doesn't help us make sense of this right-brain realm. We say, "I am angry," so this implies that anger is "who we are." A more accurate description would be "I have anger" or more specifically "Right now I have anger in me, but this will pass soon and be replaced by another feeling. Anger is not something that defines me, it's just passing through."

If we were able to be with emotions and thoughts in this way we wouldn't be so scared of the bad ones, and so saddened by the passing of the good ones. We'd be able to experience everything objectively, more with curiosity than with fear.

So if "who we are" is the spirit, not the mind, and the spirit is intangible, how can we truly know ourselves? This is where we have to go looking for clues in the energy.

The ancient Greeks had a good system for defining energy. They used archetypes (from the Greek arche typos - first type.) An archetype is a template, like a stencil through which energy can flow. This gives it a certain shape or style. We can see archetypes emerging in young children who have a natural affinity with certain behaviors. On the playground, warriors will assert themselves physically, nurses will look after friends who fall over, judges will have a sense of fair play, artistes might dream in the corner while entrepreneurs trade with items from their lunch box.

So far so good... the problem comes, as always, with the mind. There is a part of the mind that is always trying to feel safe, always trying to get more, be more, have more. As soon as one of our natural behaviors wins approval, recognition or love, the mind wants to create a strategy around the behavior and repeat it constantly. If every adult in the room applauds when we add 2 plus 2 to make 4, this could lead to an obsessive Math addiction. While our contemporaries are playing pirates we would be attempting to get our heads around calculus (the logic being *if they clap for sums, let's go for the standing ovation.*)

This is frequently how a natural talent morphs into a role or personality trait. Now the personality becomes "who we are." Instead of describing us as funny or sweet, observers say, "he's a comic," or "she's a princess."

Our spirit doesn't like to be fused to such a narrow definition (after all this was just one emerging aspect of our consciousness not the whole shebang.)

If our creative spirit is squashed or narrowly defined in this way, a couple of things can happen.

Option A

We wake up on some significant birthday (30/40/50) and declare "this is not who I am!" We give up our lucrative profession as a corporate lawyer and...

- Go off to the desert to find ourselves
- Start a school in Latin America
- Take up bungee jumping

Option B

We wake up on some significant birthday (30/40/50) and declare "this is not who I am!" We then realize we have a mortgage, kids and other commitments so we decide we can't possibly do anything about this revelation. Some unfortunate consequences of this...

- Illness – the body doesn't cope well when the spirit is gone
- Self medication – alcohol, food and recreational drugs rule
- Affairs – the last ditch attempt to feel alive
- Avatars – life is over but we can build a virtual secondary one

There's no right or wrong in any of these, they are just coping strategies for a crushed spirit. Some noble strategies, like becoming a savior of the environment (Option A) are as ineffective as some low level ones, like becoming a loquacious bar fly (Option B). This is because they are both roles. Actions that are performed from a role don't bring lasting joy because the energy behind them is out of alignment.

Now we're back to the intangible… energy! If we want access to the creative life we need to differentiate between two types of energy.

The energy of the spirit – constant, inexhaustible and high voltage.

The energy of the body (adrenaline) – none of the above.

When we're in a role we use the wrong energy. This is why our best intentions don't seem to come to fruition.

So, how do we get out of a role? We need to track back to our early natural behaviors, discover the ones that were obvious and the other talents in the wings, waiting their turn. We need to hook them up to the energy of the spirit, and let them fly. When we're naturally good at what we do and we're aligned with our energy source, we become "present."

One of the things that used to amaze me (back in the rock and roll days) was the way an average looking boy with no confidence or social grace could strap on a guitar and become transformed into a girl magnet. It had nothing to do with status. It was presence.

When we do something we love doing, we get out of our own way. Our role collapses and what we're left with, however briefly, is a glimpse of the spirit. Of course it is possible for someone with a decent left-brain strategy to become a rock star, but when this is done as a role, the results are usually very short lived. It's the difference between an X factor wannabee and Carlos Santana. When Carlos is on stage he is so far out of his own way he seems lost in the music. When he plays guitar it is a spiritual practice not an attention seeking strategy. He's at one, with himself, with the moment, with the other band members, in service to the audience and to the muse.

The same is true of all good leaders. Somehow when we see someone in the flow of creative energy it allows us an escape from our own roles. We put aside our personal strategies. We become more open hearted, more in tune with other people. This is spirituality in action. We focus less on ourselves - and the hidden agenda of asserting our individuality - and we become one with the spirit in everyone else. We're all lined up in mutual service to the task in hand. And it feels great.

But then disaster! We leave this space and our roles take over again. We don't want to be a team player anymore; we want everyone to recognize that our part in whatever project we are working on is the most important, the most valuable. Far from being "in the Now" we are in a state of continuous partial attention – one eye on the task in hand and one eye on our personal agenda.

For the past 500 years in the western world, we have been living in a capitalist society. This ideology is all about having the right to control our own life. One of the arguments of capitalism is that ownership is good because things that are communally owned are not respected. We value things that we own.

The creative spirit has a bit of a problem with both control and ownership!

Our talents, both the ones we have realized and the ones that are waiting in the wings are soul gifts. Our mind wants to capitalize on these gifts. After all, if we can make money with our talent, then we can really value it.

The spirit is the interface between the universe and our mind.

The soul is the interface between the universe and our heart.

The spirit receives inspiration and the soul gives that out to the world via creative expression. In this way thought becomes form.

So far so good. However there's a funny little paradox where the soul is concerned. Our soul doesn't belong to just us. It is also part of the collective soul of all humanity - a bit like the drop of water, which is simultaneously part of the whole ocean.

To engage in free and spontaneous creative expression we need to unhook ourselves from our capitalist ideology. This enables us to do two radical things.

- We stop trying to control our creative spirit
- We stop trying to "own" our soul gifts.

Paradoxically, once we do this, the energy starts flowing more freely. We hoard less and we contribute more. What's the point of having an attic full of dusty old art? Where's the joy in spending our entire life acting out a role?

It's no wonder we find it so hard to "know ourselves". The voice of the creative spirit is subtle and inclusive. It's trying to make itself heard, but it's usually drowned out by the voice of the ego. That'll be the one refusing to leave the stage, singing loudly and out of tune - no doubt a karaoke version of *My Way*.

Frank Sinatra's Fanfare for the Role Playing Man.

It's a mute point

DAY TWELVE

Two more days before we head back to the airport! Chloe and I are sitting on the balcony. I'm trying to type but the sun is so bright it's difficult to see the screen. Apparently it's snowing in Zermatt, where Jack Sparrow sits, not replying to his emails. Yesterday, Chloe considered cancelling her plane ticket home and driving over to visit him. She would arrive in Jack's village unannounced (looking tanned and toned from all the mountain hikes). He would have no option but to see her and confront his feelings, both positive and negative. Today she's not so sure. Neither of us have any warm clothing. The dramatic image of her confident entrance is replaced by a scene from Les Miserables in which Chloe arrives on stage shivering in flip-flops and a thin cardigan.

Self-help adage No. 12 Who would I be without my story?

Writing about archetypes leads naturally on to the reason for their existence – i.e. what kind of story are they telling? What kind of play are they acting out? After all, it's one thing to be able to identify our natural talents and characteristics but what is the purpose in all this?

Most people embarking on a creative journey will come across the following two questions.

Who am I?

What is my purpose?

In the same way that the question "Who am I?" gets distorted by the mind into a series of roles and personality traits; the question "What is my purpose in all this?" gets similarly misinterpreted. To the mind, the word "purpose" is a verb – in other words it is a "doing" word. It looks like an awful lot of activity.

People who rise early, tackle a list of goals and don't stop for a second before it's time to fall into bed, are considered "purposeful." Unfortunately this doesn't give a lot of time for self-reflection or tuning in to where the energy is and where it wants to direct us. This often means that a lot of their activity is just that... it doesn't achieve very much.

If the energy is going downstream and we are trying to swim upstream against the current, at the end of the day we can be sure we haven't been sidetracked. We may pride ourselves on our determination, but exactly how far have we travelled? To compound the problem we are often too tired to reflect on this strategy, so we get up the following day and repeat the exercise with greater focus and concentration. We defy the current even further by leaping! Pretty soon, like exhausted salmon we arrive at the top of the stream shouting, "I achieved my purpose" and immediately die.

The spirit, being energy, is connected to "all that is" and has a different idea of purpose for the human being - a more collective one. There is a bigger story going on above the sub plots of our individual dramas. This is the story of evolution to a higher state of consciousness. It includes all of us. The specific talents and skills we need are already assigned to enable us to achieve our part with ease and grace. Whilst playing this individual part, we will also feel the exhilaration of being connected to all the other players so that the experience of their joy becomes inseparable from our own.

Doesn't this sound wonderful? Wouldn't you want to be in this play?

However... meanwhile, back in the brain, our ego mind has its own version of this epic vision. Like some despot director, the ego decides it can write a much better script, be a far superior casting agent and play the central character – the one with the most lines. As far as roles go, the ego doesn't care if it's the hero or the villain, as long as it has the most screen time and therefore the most attention from the audience.

I remember my first trip to France. It was during my Pre-Raphaelite damsel years. I was in love with Jean Paul Sartre so wanted to turn myself into Simone de Beauvoir. Unfortunately I didn't have the intellect to understand most of her writings, so I contented myself with frequenting the cafes of St Germain du Pres drinking black coffee and smoking Gitanes. The most significant emotion I can recall is one of frustration. Here I was in my black clothes, with my angst filled concern for the human condition, looking the absolute picture of cool - but there was no one there to witness it. The irony!

Unrequited self love... the love that dares not speak its name.

The ancient Greeks had a name for this phenomenon – narcissism. Its meaning is conveyed by the following story.

Narcissus was a beautiful boy whose mother was told he would live to an old age as long as he did not see his reflection. She therefore took the obvious precaution of removing all mirrors from his vicinity. One day while walking in the woods he stopped to drink water from a lake, saw his own reflection and fell in love. He could not move away from the object of his affection and so died at the waters edge.

Greek stories are wonderful because they use metaphors, which create a bridge between two interpretations – the literal (lower consciousness) one and the spiritual (higher consciousness) one. On a literal level, this is a stupid boy, if he can't tell the difference between a watery image and a real person. On a metaphysical level, this is what we all do every day. All form is energy (it doesn't look like energy but now that we have magnifying glasses we know that everything is vibrating molecules.) We "see" this energy according to the lenses in our own eyes... and then we fall in love.

That's why the phrase "I don't know what she sees in him" is so unhelpful. When we "see" things according to our projections, we become enchanted. So how could Narcissus's mother have changed the outcome of her son's story?

As Einstein said, you can't solve a problem with the same level of thinking that created it. In other words you have to leave the literal world and go to a higher level of consciousness. Here, images and symbolic language are more important than words because there is less room for misinterpretation.

Narcissus needed to find his essence, his true self, not his ego identity or role. He needed to recognize the spirit within. Having done this, he would have projected a different image onto the water but he would also have the inner sense to understand that he was connected to both the image and the water that contained it. It is this inner sense or innocence that Jesus referred to when he advised, "becoming like little children." He didn't mean become sentimental, stubborn or naïve (the interpretation of some of his followers), he meant devoid of projections so that the reflection we see is one we can live with. One in which we can live. This would have saved Narcissus's life.

So, how do we unhook from our projections, realize our true essence, recognize our natural talents, plug into the energy of the creative spirit and step up?!

Back to the individual story we are telling...

If we are going to stand in the spotlight we have to realize that light casts shadows. Unless we are comfortable with these shadows, we will never have the courage to walk across the stage.

All great stories have sub plots or back-stories. They give the narration more depth, texture and added interest. The hero of the story has to have something to fight against, villains to overcome, wrong paths to avoid. The bigger story of our evolution has the same dynamic. Our adversaries are the shadows created by the light. We can't capture them. We can't kill them off. We somehow have to befriend and integrate them.

Who would we be without our stories? Shadow boxing consumes such a lot of time and energy. It's reasonable to assume that if we were released from this daily workout we could channel that time and energy into something much more creative!

Narcissus

DAY THIRTEEN

It was all going so well with Chloe's letting go process. Perhaps too well!

First there was Simon Cowell, the record company mogul in the UK, whose details she dramatically deleted from her Blackberry. Then, she realized the folly of holding onto the threads of Jack Sparrow and her need for "closure" so she let him go as well. Now comes the setback! Having realized that the plan to drive to Zermatt was not a good idea, she faces the prospect of returning to the UK with no beau to appreciate her tanned, toned body. Unless...

Perhaps things are not quite over with Simon Cowell! After all he did send her a very nice email. The fact that he addressed the message "My dear friend" and not "Woman of my dreams who I still have the hots for" does not bode well, but we don't want to engage in negative thinking. The universe is vastly intelligent and has the means to turn these things around. Chloe has now gone for a long walk in order to look for a sign...

Despite my analogy of life being a play while we are the actors, I'm not quite so confident that any meaningful stage direction will come from the forces of nature. It's at times like these that you could really do with a shaman or a witchdoctor. The problem with the symbolic realm is the difficulty of the interpretation. It's like trying to make sense of dreams.

It's much more practical to interpret the energy... at least you can feel that, so there's less room for misinterpretation.

So how would we draw the energy map of a person?!

Self-help adage No. 13 The map is not the territory

We have known for a long time what the body's physical map looks like. Anatomy books are full of intriguing, colorful charts. There's the one with the blood vessels, all red and blue tributaries. Another page shows the nervous system with its tiny fine lines weaving in and out of the surrounding mountains of muscle and beneath it all the deep foundations of the skeletal system. There's a whole world going on inside our body.

If we're going to map the energetic equivalent, this map would probably resemble one of the meteorological charts that weather men stand in front of, only there would be a whole lot more going on than a little light precipitation.

How to map the energetic vibration of thoughts and emotions?

Some people like to separate them into two teams. They like to have a "side" they support. Often women favor emotion (more empathic and caring) and men favor thought (more logical and strategic). Both are necessary and together they are powerful. When they are separated however, it doesn't bode well for the weather.

Without the focus and strategic direction of thought, emotion is just a vortex of energy that sucks in everything in its path - at best ineffective, at worst destructive. Without the energy of emotion, thoughts have little power to turn ideas into action.

An emotion is like a spinning top. In order to keep it going, it needs a "twist" every now and then. A thought is the twist that keeps it going. Yesterday, Chloe sat with her emotions and just focused on them until they ran out of energy. Eventually the spinning slowed down and almost came to a stop but then disaster! Thoughts came! They sounded something like this...

"I have let go of both boyfriends in order to find Mr. Right... or in order for Mr. Right to find me, now that I have successfully created a vacuum for the universe to fill. But what if the law of magnetic attraction is a lie? What if Mr. Right doesn't come along, and in the intervening time I have lost my option of 'Mr. Almost Right' and what if by the time I realize Mr. Right is not coming along, it will be too late to ever get married and have children... then I'll be unhappy for ever."

Now the top is spinning like crazy! If we try to reach out for it, it just shoots off in another direction. It's like a runaway train. Nothing can stop it. The anxiety collects fear, the fear collects more thoughts that reinforce the worst-case scenario... and on it goes. This is the dysfunctional union of thought and emotion. It's like a very bad marriage. So what would a good one look like?

Everyone knows how difficult it is to direct something that is spinning out of control with negative thoughts. Logically we think we can slow the spin with some positive thoughts but the vortex, once created, consumes everything in its path and the positive thoughts get spat out, like bits of debris discarded by the whirling hurricane as it whizzes along.

A good marriage of thought and emotion requires feeling. Feelings run deeper than emotions. In order to feel at this depth, we have to be willing to open our heart; to move our awareness there; to sense heart wisdom rather than brain knowledge. This creates a different channel for the energy to move along. The image resembles a double helix rather than a spinning top. The energy weaves in and out and up and down our spine in a continuous infinity loop. This takes a little practice. We are more familiar with an energetic map of emotions because we're hard wired for the intensity of drama and adrenaline. They make us feel alive.

We prefer the spectacle of crashing waves on the surface, to the mysteries of the ocean depths. If we're serious about creativity however, we would be wise to become intimate with this deeper place within us.

My boyfriend (more on him later!) was once in an actual hurricane. It started with an enormous storm that uprooted trees and sent cars somersaulting across the road like bits of tumbleweed. When it passed away there was an eerie silence and in that silence he realized there was a presence of "something else", an energy that he could not identify, because it was outside his normal frame of reference. After a while he realized that the storm had not passed and that he was in fact sitting in the eye of the storm.

The only way to stop an emotion that is spinning out of control, one that is being flicked constantly by negative thoughts, is to dive right into the center of it. This takes a little faith and willingness but at the center there is help. At the center a new dimension of consciousness shows up. One that allows us to slow the spinning down. One that allows us to see the storm from a different perspective. If we sit in the center and have the willingness to be present, the emotion runs out of energy, slows and eventually stops for good.

We have to work from the inside out. It's a different perspective... yet another lens for *the Sextant*.

Meanwhile, back in the physical world, Chloe is back from her walk. She saw a stag, a bright red butterfly and a funny shaped rock formation that could have been... well anything really. She is still no clearer about her feelings for Simon and how her body will respond when she meets him again. She has a map of London so it would be fairly easy to avoid the locations he frequents. However she knows hurricanes have little respect for maps – they tend to carve out their territory with reckless abandon.

"Aaaarrgghhh!! Why is it all so difficult" she yells.

I suggest that, it being Saturday night, it was probably time to give up metaphysics and drink large quantities of red wine.

But on the other hand, as someone once remarked... "People who drown their sorrows should be aware, that sorrow knows how to swim."

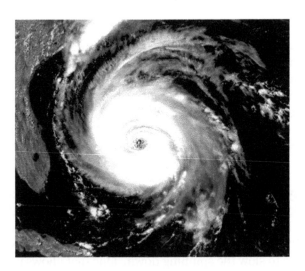

You spin me right round baby right round like a record baby round round round round

DAY FOURTEEN

Self-help adage No. 14 **Live in the Now**

Last day here! Well, not strictly day as it is in fact the middle of the night. I have raging insomnia again and have given up trying to sleep. Perhaps it's the silence, or the darkness. When the chalet shutters are closed it is pitch black. I get up and walk outside. There are a million tiny stars but no moon. My thoughts are an incomprehensible jumble of half finished sentences. I wonder what it would be like to live in a monastery for an entire lifetime, just being with the constant silence. Would it make it easier to pray or more difficult?

It is said that Helen Keller developed her ability to live in a silent, sightless world. Being both blind and deaf, she could sense a person by their vibration. If someone entered the room, years after meeting her, she would recognize them through the energy they vibrated. Perhaps by relying so heavily on our five senses, we disallow these extraordinary senses to grow. Not only do we rely on our five senses but we saturate them with added stimulation - constant noise, ubiquitous advertising and hundreds of food choices in a 24/7 environment with dwindling personal space (particularly if we have to travel by public transport in the rush hour).

No wonder we have become desensitized. We have more choices than ever, yet nothing looks, feels, sounds, or tastes the way we imagine it should. We go on holiday to places that don't quite capture the high definition experience of watching them on television. We buy things that lose their desirability by the time we have discarded the packaging. Restaurants compete for our custom with innovative new menus. Retail stores tempt us with sophisticated brands. And still we don't know what we want.

We want something good.

We instinctively know we are not satisfied. We consume more and more but still the yearning is not sated. We look like smart, sophisticated, successful people but we're no better than Pre-Raphaelite damsels, waiting to be rescued by the latest technology from Apple. In the same way that Coca Cola appropriated the St Nicholas story to become the jolly red stocking filler, Steve Jobs is the new Sir Lancelot liberating us from ennui and unattractive suitors.

The problem is not with the stuff; the problem lies with our capacity to appreciate things. We need to upgrade our senses. When I walked in the forest yesterday I missed countless things that a trained eye would have noticed. Likewise I can hear perfectly well but I don't really listen, there isn't enough space in my head because of all those thoughts that keep me awake in the middle of the night.

In the story of our evolution, this could be where we are headed – extra sensory beings with an entirely different perceptual system. Imagine if we could all read the energy in the same way that Helen Keller and the enlightened mystics could.

This would be a paradigm shift worth waiting for. If we could "see through" everything, via our heightened senses, there would be true transparency. This would change everything. There would be no hiding behind spin. Politicians, Bankers, Corporations would have no option but to tell the truth – because what they *really* thought would be apparent in the spinning wheels of their energy system. Romantic relationships would certainly be different. The "What's the matter?"... "Nothing" conversation would cease to be an option in marital dialogues. And as for our relationships with work colleagues, we would certainly see how effective all those bonding, team-building sessions really are!

Most significant of all would be a new understanding of our own energy system. There would be no hiding place for the internal "spinning tops" we don't own up to. No refuge for the less attractive archetypes we hide in the basement when people come to call; our angry, vindictive, jealous selves; our guilt ridden, shame filled shadows. The basement would have a glass ceiling!

Transparency could actually be quite liberating. Given a choice between an honest, angry, jealous person and a false, nice, kind person, we all prefer the former. We love it when our leaders have the humility to admit their failings. It gives us permission to come clean about ours.

I was educated in a catholic convent where the nuns were constantly praying and going to confession. I often wondered what they had to confess and why they prayed. They lived such blame free lives and had so few requirements – a new prayer book perhaps, a rosary or an extra blanket?

I thought it ironic that they had so little to pray for and so much time in which to do it. I now realize that time was irrelevant to them; that they were all about being in a relationship with "presence" and being in the present moment, where "presence" lives. They say one moment of pure presence is worth a lifetime of good deeds - that if you experience it, even for a moment, you want to spend your whole lifetime getting back there.

We on the other hand, with our busy lives, pray for more time to do all the things we want to do - find romantic love, accomplish our goals and achieve success. We live everywhere but the present moment. We live in regrets about the past and hopes about the future. And while all that's going on we completely miss the present.

I remember watching my children when they were little, having the most brilliant, creative, fun filled time. They were completely absorbed in the "now." I could have joined them, but rather than realizing the wonderful gift on offer, I was anywhere but in the "now." I was wondering when we needed to leave, what time the park was going to close, whether there was any food in the fridge for dinner, if I should go to the supermarket on the way home or drop them off first... endless, meaningless thoughts that stole the far superior present moment, right from under my eyes.

The next dial on *The Sextant* has to assist with the uncoupling from this magnetic pull - the power of beliefs from the past. It has to provide encouragement for "Living in the Now." Courage comes from the French 'Coeur' meaning heart. This dial is not for the left-brain. We cannot enter the "Now" through the mind; we can only get there if we have the courage to open our heart.

As I look at the starry, starry night, it's impossible not to feel awestruck by the vastness of it all, impossible not to feel reverence. Something inside us resonates with the incalculable size. This too is beyond the parameters of the mind. I realize I have been sitting here for some time without the want of anything. In this moment of noticing myself for the first time I suddenly feel cold and hungry. My mind, having been temporarily suspended, has kicked back in. But I'm grateful for the peace and I understand the monks a little more.

Dawn is breaking and I can hear Chloe bustling about in the kitchen. My limbs are aching from the cold and my senses intoxicated by the smell of coffee as I become conscious of my body. Chloe is dressed in the funniest arrangement of random clothing. She can make any outfit look exotic and fabulous. I wonder whether to suggest we do our next writing holiday in a monastery. Watching her navigate the coffee machine in the makeshift mittens provided by her stripy socks, I couldn't quite imagine her as a cloistered Nun.

French boys would don black armbands, the world would be a less colorful place, and the Now would be robbed of its perfect moment. As Oscar Wilde wisely put it, 'Be yourself... everyone else is already taken'.

Vincent's starry, starry night

DAY FIFTEEN

It's time to make the journey home. The two weeks have passed quickly and it seems impossible that tomorrow we will wake up in rainy London with no incredible mountain view and no magical forest walks. Last night we went into the near empty village for our last meal, expecting to see the usual handful of locals. In fitting irony (there having been no men under the age of 70 during our entire stay) we were greeted by an entire delegation of French rugby players who presumably were up in the mountains for high altitude training purposes. Chloe was appreciated and joyful, and we drank too much red wine as we pondered the meaning of this sign.

Self-help adage No. 15 The universe is abundant

This morning of course we feel less perky as we have to clean and vacate the chalet with hangovers. After handing the keys back, we decide to go for one last walk.

It's a cliché but nature actually is incredible. I'm slowly starting to understand the adage "the map is not the territory." How could a map encompass everything that is really going on? It limits things to statistics - the height of trees, width of rivers, composition of soil, density of rock. Yet within and between all this, is a complex wonderland where everything works in perfect harmony. New things emerge from the dying embers of previous glory. Life just happens without any assistance whatsoever. Animals, birds, minerals, vegetation all organize themselves according to some psychic blueprint - without any help from an advanced left-brain.

Of course the landscaped gardens of someone like Capability Brown are an incredible feat of engineering, but they don't come close to this harmony, created without any human assistance whatsoever. It's why artistes, poets and mystics have used nature as their inspiration for centuries. There is spirit in each element of nature, each leaf, rock, or droplet of water in a stream - something beyond the structure contained by the map. It's the presence contained by this "spirit of the thing" that inspires us.

Unlike man-made forms, nature is not static; it vibrates at a frequency beyond our understanding. We can't comprehend this because we are trying to understand it with our mind. Our mind is like a detective, always breaking things down looking for hard evidence, but the more we look with our mind, the less we see. We can only become aware of the true magic of nature if we use another sense – one that requires a different level of consciousness.

Trying to fathom the beauty of life with our mind is like trying to understand the taste of a peach without any taste buds. We could describe it with words, we could draw a picture but without the necessary sense (taste) it would be impossible to actually experience it.

Similarly we come unstuck in our creative journey because we are often trying to create something that makes sense to our logical mind. The more effort we put in, the more elusive is the experience of creativity. In fact "creative journey" is an oxymoron. The spirit doesn't need a journey in order to be creative. It's more a matter of remaining still and slowly dissolving the illusions, thoughts and beliefs that block the awareness of our creativity. The tap is always on.

But therein lies yet another paradox! To be perfectly still but not static! To be at peace, while vibrating at a very high frequency.

Nature shows us incredible lessons. In order to gain a bird in the hand, it is completely ineffective to chase after it. The best method is to stand very still with some very good birdseed and the bird will be attracted to us. This involves a lot less movement and action on our part. It also necessitates that we look to our inner energy (our point of attraction) to make sure this is vibrating in a good way.

But we do love our drama. Our busyness is an addiction. It looks like there's a lot of stuff going on, so it makes us feel purposeful. We rarely check to see the efficacy of all that action. I was once asked by another of my teachers, Chuck Spezzano, why I *didn't* want peace. (Turning questions around like this, often gives insight into the sub conscious). The conscious mind wants to say "but of course I want peace, why would I not want peace." However quick as a flash my subconscious mind said, "Because it would be so boring."

This is our universal belief, and it is a flawed one.

Real peace, the "peace of the spirit" is thrilling. It is "peace of mind" that can be boring. Our mind doesn't want peace because it would be without a job and nobody likes to feel redundant.

Rather reluctantly Chloe and I tear ourselves away from Arcadia, and start walking back to the little car. A flock of birds pass overhead. With winter approaching, they too are on their way to a different country. With no GPS and a brain the size of a small pea, they will reach their destination right on time. It's easy to forget that there is intelligence far beyond our comprehension and far more capable of coping with complexity than all our left-brains put together. The birds move in perfect formation, changing direction at exactly the same time without the need for rehearsals or extensive choreography.

Being part of nature, humans are no different. We are wired up to be aware of ourselves as one species, just like swarms of bees, shoals of fish or herds of wildebeest. It's just that we have a pesky neo cortex, which gets in the way of our connectedness. We try to impose our will on our surroundings. We think we're so smart, but as Gregory Bateson says "Nature doesn't work the way man thinks."

The most tragic example of this took place in China in 1958 when Mao Tse-Tung ordered the killing of sparrows, who were eating the grain seeds. Over a two year period the Chinese people obediently tore down nests, broke eggs and shot birds out of the sky. They banged pots and pans to scare them from landing until they eventually fell from the sky with exhaustion. By 1960 it became apparent that the birds ate more insects than grain seeds, however this realization came too late. The birds were almost extinct by the time the country became infested with insects including a plague of locusts, who in turn had to be attacked with insecticides.

There is vast evidence to suggest that this ecological imbalance led to the Great Chinese Famine, one of the worst disasters in Chinese history, during which time approximately 30 million people died of starvation.

Sparrows... not so insignificant after all.

We arrive at the car and set off for Perpignan airport. Chloe drives very slowly, partly out of reverence for nature and partly because we are feeling a little ill from the previous night's red wine and the road is very, very windy.

The airport is a massive reality check. It is full of aging golfers, no doubt taking advantage of the cheap flights to reduce their handicaps in the autumn sunshine. They are all talking loudly, laughing at unfunny jokes and drinking beer. We are typing away on our laptops, being purposeful and highly judgmental. It is difficult to maintain a spiritual perspective when surrounded by sticky tables, neon lighting and people in unattractive clothing.

Once we reach London, our journey home is hampered by cancelled trains due to signal failure. Waterloo station lacks the charm once captured by Ray Davies and the Kinks or perhaps he had a more constant relationship with the muse. *"As long as I gaze on Waterloo sunset, I am in paradise."* We, on the other hand, are exhausted and cold, as we stand in a sea of discarded free newspapers and watch the clattering departure board showing trains to every destination but our own.

Paradise seems an awful long way away.

Waterloo station

DAY SIXTEEN

At last some sleep. There's nothing like your own bed to dispel demons and strangeness. I sit at the computer to start the day's writing but am overwhelmed by the email mountain that greets me. Two weeks without Wi-Fi has its disadvantages. Amongst the various missives, the following dramas are revealed:

1. I am being fined $400 for not "filing a document" concerning my tax code on time. After phoning to advise that there was no tax due (having been in penury this past year) I am told that the fine is not related to "non payment" just "non filing." Filing, apparently in the eyes of the tax department, has nothing to do with the placing of paperwork in folders underneath the desk.

2. My landline phone has been cut off. This means that the 30 minutes I was on hold to the tax department from a cell phone has probably just cost me as much money as my holiday in France.

These are just two irritating examples of the endless exasperating incidents we all have to deal with on a daily basis. Sorting out administrative problems without going crazy now requires either a frontal lobotomy or the patience of a saint. It's impossible to speak to a person without listening to four or five recorded messages. Between these is the "on hold" music. At various stages the requirement to key in specific numbers becomes strangely difficult when lulled into a trance by an electronic xylophone version of Greensleeves. If we press the wrong digit a default message comes up and we are forced to start the whole process all over again "I'm sorry we cannot understand your request... goodbye." It's the happy tone of the "goodbye" that has caused so much collateral damage. As we rip the door from its hinges two thoughts occur.

1. I have building insurance

2. If I want to claim, I have to go through this whole procedure again.

This is why we have given up complaining – we have no outlet. We put up with rubbish service, unfair parking tickets, incorrect bills, spurious additional charges, all because the process involved in taking any form of action causes more damage to our health than smoking. It is this gradual wearing down of our psyche by petty irritations that we struggle with, not the big things. We long for the big things.

Creativity is a big thing.

Self-help adage No. 16 Don't sweat the small stuff

It's easy for someone who has "staff" to say this. Delegate and get on with the things that matter. It's pretty difficult these days to find anyone who classes themselves as a secretary. It gives us some clue to the fact that nobody wants to sweat any small stuff - their own or anybody else's. No one wants to do the filing.

In my last advertising job the situation had become so chronic that there had been no filing done for over a year – everyone was too busy being in meetings. Consequently no one could find anything. The server was chock a block full of folders of unsorted work. My son was on holiday from university at the time and was in his words "broke as a joke" so I suggested he could go in and do the filing. Not only did they pay him, but he also achieved near legendary status within two months. Even after he was back at university he was still receiving emails and directing people to the relevant information. It wasn't that he was Einstein but in a supply and demand market, over populated with media consultants and marketing specialists, you could find that being a good filing clerk carries an awful lot of power and respect.

So why do we attach so much importance to status and job titles? We need to take a closer look at what creates identity and the difference between self-esteem and soul esteem.

Self esteem, being a "mind" thing is an analytical process of comparison. It needs context. *Am I more important or less important than a colleague? Am I funnier/prettier/more successful than somebody else or am I less wealthy/attractive/popular than them.* Because there are always bigger and better people to compare ourselves to, comparison creates an endless source of discontent.

This brings us back to the "audience" thing again. The goals of the mind always require an audience for validation. *Look at me in my fabulous, important job.*

Anyone who reads celebrity magazines (scanning them at the entrance of the supermarket while waiting for a trolley *does* count) realizes how fickle an audience is. In fact most celebrities are just empty canvases for peoples projections. *I hate myself (she's thinner than me.) I love myself (I'm thinner than her.)*

This is another stress that previous generations didn't face. In the old days, our future was fixed, determined by birth and genetics. The modern premise that "anybody can re-invent themselves" brings a lot of pressure. All our excuses have been blown out of the water. With will power we can be as successful, wealthy or creative as we want to be. Bugger.

Soul esteem is the upgraded version of self-esteem and is a completely different scenario. It requires less looking out and more looking in. When we look inside there's no comparing to do, we're just competing against ourselves.

In addition to being hard wired for comparison, the mind also has a compulsion to trade – it does everything for a reason. Doing a kind thing for somebody else when nobody is there to witness it makes no sense to our mind – if we give something, we expect something back (even though we may not be conscious of this.) The mind needs its identity validated and endorsed at all times.

The soul plays a completely different game with different laws. Being energy, it knows we are all connected. Therefore anything we do for another, we in fact do for ourselves. If we do something with a hidden agenda, we only cheat ourselves.

This is a tricky premise to argue. Despite the fact that we've seen all the science documentaries, and we know that we are made up of interconnecting molecules, our mind wants to believe we are separate. We are! Quantum physics has revealed that at a micro level everything can be a wave or a particle at the same time. Similarly we are a spirit and a body. Our soul rules our spirit and our mind rules our body. As our mind doesn't want us to understand this paradox, it creates a smokescreen of drama, comparison and trading. Mystics can transcend this level of perception, but for most of us mere mortals, it takes a dramatic event to break the spell.

When a man risked his own life to haul a suicide jumper back from the Brooklyn Bridge, the news reporters questioned his sanity – after all the victim was a complete stranger. Instead of the "Someone's gotta be a hero" response, he described a "Damascene Moment" in which he saw that the person on the bridge was himself. There was no separation. He was saving his own life. He also said that in that moment, time stood still. He had, in a flash, accessed the world beyond the veil of illusion; the world beyond time; the Now; the space between the atoms. He was using a different perceptual system – one far greater than the five senses we limit ourselves to. Rather than being a heroic act it was "a no brainer." (Certainly a no left-brainer)

We can't detangle from small stuff and we often can't delegate our way out of it. We need to reach through the veil and start living at a higher, more creative level.

Sighing, I make a big cup of coffee and return to my desk while pondering a high level approach to re-arranging the molecules of my $400 tax bill. It doesn't work, so I open my heart and send a lovely letter to the inspector of taxes, pleading stupidity and asking for lenience. After all... he is me.

Paper round

DAY SEVENTEEN

I have not written a word of *the Sextant* for two days. I've managed to tame my paper mountain but there are so many other things that claim my attention before I can think about being creative.

"Think" is the operative word here. Thinking hypnotizes us into paralysis. Some people rent an office to do their creative work, the argument being that there are fewer distractions in a new space and a "work" environment is more conducive to productivity. However all my distractions are in my head so they'd just come along with me. I can spend hours thinking about my "to do" list then wondering why nothing gets ticked off, apart from myself of course.

Nike capitalized on this flaw and turned it into a brand – *Just do it.* For a while this felt positive and upbeat. We listened to Tony Robbins and felt positive and dynamic. Tony's workshops are full of people punching the air like Masters of the Universe. The universe is mainly smiling like an indulgent parent. *How sweet – they think they can control time and space from where they are.* This is a bit like making a cup of coffee without entering the kitchen first.

We can't *think* about being creative (unless we want to make ourselves miserable.) Our mind will just kick back (both versions – fighting and laying on the couch). We can't *Just do it* (unless we want to push more adrenaline into a stressed body.) Our mind and body want a familiar pattern, not an unknown mystery. We need to stop thinking and doing and start working with the energy, start taming the emotions at the edge of the storm so we can fall into the center where the real power lies.

Let's see how Chloe is doing! She had a response from Simon Cowell who says he has a "window" in five days time. Very busy successful people allocate their time through panes of glass. Chloe is allocating hers on a large whiteboard, which maps out a killer regime including multiple gym sessions and the eating of broccoli (and little else).

I feel the urge to caution her about the managing of expectations but don't have the heart to burst her joyous bubble. I too have had a meaningful relationship with the damsel archetype. It's easy to judge, but when you're addicted to intense feelings, it's difficult to see the value in predictable people. The emotional patterns in the Knight/Damsel are created by the extreme polarity of their psyches.

The Knight is very left-brain - strategies and battles. He guards his heart (hence the protective shield) because he's uncomfortable with feelings. Honor and status are important. He likes jousting and quests and the things of the mind. The longer he keeps his heart locked away, the more arid his life becomes. Knights frequently die in deserts. Literal ones (the Crusades) and symbolic ones (the Office).

The Damsel is very right-brain - emotion and feeling. She has little time for logic and likes to be swept away by the power of love. The damsel doesn't have emotions; emotions have the damsel. She simply has no control over them. She is lured, as if by sirens, to swim in their waters. When the sea is peaceful she floats and fantasizes. When it is turbulent, she relies on the knight to pull her out. If he doesn't arrive on time she can drown in her own neediness.

I remember planning "the big night" with a successful and therefore very "time poor" boyfriend. Two days of preening and attention to detail. Dilemmas about what to wear, and more importantly what to wear underneath what to wear. Finally the day arrived and after a brief romantic dinner, his jet lag kicked in and he fell asleep. There I was, drugged on adrenaline and expectation, exfoliated to within an inch of my life and he couldn't even see me – his window was closed.

Chloe... don't do it! Stop! Step away from the pedicure!

I have children. They don't listen either. Sadly, we all have to learn by experience. My personal learning curve (on the way to becoming an adult) was more of a circle. I started off (like most of us) with the neediness of the Child. This deepened to the neediness of the Victim when I came face to face with teenage angst.

At the bottom of the curve I made a huge leap into "I don't need anybody." I was ultra cool in my isolation and judged all people I considered to be "un-cool". Here my relationship with the Prostitute was forged. Everything was a power negotiation. If someone had more power, I would sell pieces of my soul for their approval. If someone had less power, they would not even show up on my radar so could be inadvertently crushed.

Eventually I ended up in the desert with the Saboteur. He was the only one still talking to me. I was sitting in a fortress, surrounded by sand bags, thirsty, bored and lonely and wondering why nothing felt exciting or fun any more. Sometimes people start the long walk back to the center from here. Mostly they're scared to do this. There are people we've been mean to, hiding in the dunes. Usually - like the guy on the Brooklyn Bridge - it takes an incident to force us to leave the fortress while we're still alive.

My damascene moment came in one hit. In new age parlance, after gentle taps on the shoulder from my guardian angel, (which I could not feel through my bulletproof vest), I was whacked with the cosmic 4 x 2. It's something I don't recommend to anyone and now that I love all those people hiding in the dunes (after all, they are me!) it's quite appropriate that I devise a tool to help people leave the bunker and head for Middle Earth in the center.

Life should be creative. If we refuse this challenge, life tends to get very painful. Our heart is meant to be open. If we close the door, it's likely to get knocked down. It's called a natural disaster. Don't you just love the universe? It usually gets its own way.

Self-help adage No. 17 Surrender

Chloe meanwhile is trying to make peace with the tsunami of her emotions. She has lit a candle and sacrificed a goat (I lied about the goat - it doesn't go well with the broccoli). She knows that under the role of the damsel lies all her neediness and yearning, which comes from a sense of lack. She has to become her own knight and vanquish the dragon that sits on the inner treasure of her creativity. There is no "lack" except in the mind and the mind is nothing compared to the spirit. This feels like a much better image. More "Joan of Arc" than "Lady of Shallot." She will banish the neediness by seeing through its disguise. After all, it is just a thought form.

And she has a sword.

When my life capsized, I fell into a terrible depression. Fellow sufferers will recognize the symptoms - constant exhaustion, and the temptation that drowning would be so much easier. Instead I went to my first self-help workshop where I met Chuck Spezzano. I was feeling particularly forlorn and damsel like, but he had an entirely different take on depression. He said it was "anger without the enthusiasm." This description is just so brilliant. If you can somehow find the anger in your condition you can fight. And once you're fighting you can get some hope. If you can feel hope you can reach enthusiasm. If you can get a bit of enthusiasm going a hand reaches out for you and pulls you the rest of the way up.

The word enthusiasm comes from "en theos" - "in God." This is our destination. This is the creative realm in the eye of the storm. If we're on the sidelines (the left or right camps of the Knight and the Damsel) we have to fight the flak of emotional debris in order to get in. If we're under the basement trapdoor of depression, we have to push our way up. But this is where we're headed.

Like Harrison Ford stepping onto the bridge we have to trust this invisible realm. There is something powerful in empty space, something that won't let us fall. It just requires that we surrender. Our mind interprets the word "surrender" as giving up - defeat after a fight. Our heart would probably conjure an image of freedom.

One of the inspiring parts of David Attenborough's documentaries (there are so many) is watching baby eagles take their maiden flight. They have no idea what's in store as they sit cozy in their nests, until one day the Mother Eagle pushes them out with her nose. She has the instinct to do this, as she has supreme trust that everything will be ok. The baby birds plummet, as if to their death. In their panic their wings open, the wind catches them... and they start to fly.

Chicks away!

DAY EIGHTEEN

So, no excuses left. I must crack on with the writing. All administrative malarkey is under control. The small stuff has been shoved in a stripped pine box where it is sweating away (hopefully reducing in volume).

If we want to travel to the creative realm we have to become familiar with the dynamics that operate there. We know it's all about energy and endless possibility. This could overwhelm us if we don't know how to keep our balance. We've looked at the balanced heart of the Knight/Damsel, now let's look at the balanced brain.

Self-help adage No. 18 **Step up to the plate**

There's an interesting baseball analogy that relates to the stand off between the left-brain and the right-brain. I don't know who first told it, possibly Sir Ken Robinson who has such brilliant stories about children. It goes something like this... Boys don't like girls on the baseball team. If a boy takes his third strike, misses, and starts to cry, the other boys will stick to the rules – 3 strikes and you're out. The girls will usually feel moved and want to give him another turn. This drives the boys crazy because they are already building the left-brain framework of logic. The girls meanwhile have already established their right-brain bias. In other words the boys will hurt feelings in order to save the rules and the girls will break the rules in order to save the feelings.

If we're going to climb Jacob's ladder, we need a level platform to stand it on. Our current perception of creativity is unbalanced – only right-brainers need apply and they should fit the popular stereotype by turning up late *"I have no concept of time"* and wearing funny clothes. Left-brainers, on the other hand, are tasked with all the important work like stategy, planning and organising.

Keeping the two sides apart is madness, yet most legal, educational, financial, governmental and health systems are based on this model. The left-brainers keep building impressive structures that seem to have no glue holding them together. They can only see the part they are working on. When the structure collapses the creative, intuitive, holistic people say, *"surely that was obvious."*

We need to integrate these two sides and develop a different relationship with the *source* of creativity, not the identity of creativity. Anybody who has looked at the sky on a clear night, visited a cave of crystals underground or studied the inner workings of a human being realizes that what we find complicated and unfathomable is easy for the *source* of creativity. Problems like "What if it doesn't work? Where will the money come from? How will we build it? are laugh out loud questions when you've just invented color, zebras and personalized snowflakes (the ultimate expression of creative glee.) We don't have to worry about how this will happen – we just have to step up to the plate.

So why don't we show up for baseball practice? We're still squabbling on the bench. Our inner female brain argues that the sandy path of logic leads directly to a straightjacket in a Mexican jail. Our inner male brain convinces us that the feeling path is unstable. After all you can't build stuff on top of water.

Of course if they got together, they'd come up with something like Venice.

It takes a great confidence trick to keep these polarities in place. And that's exactly what the ego is good at - its trick is to remove our confidence, (our faith) and replace it with fear. So here's how we warm up before the game. We need to stretch the parts of ourselves we haven't used, before we start playing. After all, we don't want to break anything...

Apart from our paradigm.

Integration exercise

1. Create two spaces. Advanced people can do this metaphysically (by getting in touch with the two parts of the mind) but it's easier for the rest of us rookies to do it literally i.e. take two chairs and put them opposite each other.

2. Sit in the chair on the right and start to question yourself about why you resist rules. Some ideas will start to pop into your head. Imagine a timeline so that you can start tracking backwards to earlier and earlier occasions when rules were imposed against your will, and the corresponding feelings of being disempowered. There will be unreasonable bosses, belligerent traffic wardens, incomprehensible computer software, inflexible school regulations, and strict teachers. The timeline often ends at your Dad and how you felt about him. Of course there are "good rules" that we had no problem with but these will have no "charge" so are not relevant for the purpose of this exercise.

3. Now sit in the chair on the left and start to question yourself about why you resist needy people. Again do the timeline thing. In this picture will come a motley crew of easily defeated, pathetic characters, plus some irrational, hysterical ones. In the work environment there will be victims and complainers. In relationships there will be manipulators and martyrs. At school there will be a bunch of children, who failed tests, missed open goals, were excluded from parties and clung to parents legs at the gates. It's a tough trip down memory lane - a rote of no confidence. The end of this line ends with your Mum and how you felt about her.

All these people represent parts of our spirit that we have split away from and left behind. If we replay images from the past, we can notice that when the scene ends, after we leave, part of our energy remains there, anchored to the place or person. Simultaneously part of the energy of "there" gets stuck inside us. Now the particles are entangled!

Years later, if we think about these scenes, or we encounter a similar situation, we feel a twist in our stomach – this is an indication of trapped energy. The energy acts as a black hole, pulling towards us the matching energy in other people. Suddenly we are surrounded by needy or aggressive people. It's not random or karma - it's simple magnetics.

Recap:

There are two forms of perception – left-brain and right-brain - but our default position is the usually the left. The left-brain likes to be in control. It wants to get rid of all the needy or aggressive people and make up its own rules. It's seen a lot of Clint Eastwood movies where everything is logical – shoot the bad guys, give someone a sheriff's badge and leave town. The left-brain is not holistic or long term so never has a plan for the sequel in which the bad guys' sons and nephews come back in force and the sheriff has got fat and lazy from all that good living.

The right-brain on the other hand thinks neediness is no big deal; it's just trapped energy that is trying to make its presence felt so that it can be released. At the beginning of our lives we were all helpless. The feeling wasn't a pleasant one so it's no wonder we couldn't wait to grow up. It's a drag to have to go back there, but we left bits of our energy behind and if we want to turn up to the baseball game in good shape, we need a tour bus with a full set of wheels.

Kids are always playing with chairs. In our house chairs have been everything from pirate ships to desert islands. Stakes are raised now - life is a game for grown ups too. If we want to be creative players, we need to show up, sit in the chairs, do some excavation and change the rules of the game.

The moment of truth

DAY NINETEEN

The Sextant is taking some sort of shape but my insomnia is now a nightly occurrence and I feel exhausted. Robert Palmer is on the iPod. Chloe has been trawling through the left and right parts of her brain "looking for clues." She is now facing two big challenges - one for each hemisphere, so on the plus side at least her problems are balanced.

1. Having looked at her outgoings (considerable) - this is London where a few bus trips, a cappuccino and a sandwich cost the equivalent of the average daily wage - and having looked at her income (zero) she is now panicking about the wisdom of giving up her job. Also she moves into her flat share in a week and her new landlord has taken the concept of "deposit" to new heights (how much damage can three people make?)

2. In a couple of days she is meeting up with ex boyfriend, Simon Cowell.

Real life challenges are a good opportunity for doing the left/right-brain exercise. Chloe was hoping for something a little more aerobic but is prepared to give it a go. First up... the left-brain chair.

Self-help adage No. 19 Let go of your father

Chloe's previous job was Account Executive at an advertising agency. She lists the reasons for giving it up... difficult clients, a demanding boss and long hours at the coalface, which prevented her from writing (her true destiny). The money she earned seemed to disappear as soon as it entered her bank account, so she was no better off. Her boss didn't appreciate her and was oblivious to all the effort she put in.

If we truly know ourselves to be creative, we don't need a particular job to remind us of who we are (creative beings.) Frequently people with "so called" creative jobs, don't feel any more creative than the rest of us. A far greater proportion of their day is often spent in non creative activities - pre-planning, understanding a complicated brief, taking criticism, defending the idea, re-working the idea to fit around constantly changing requirements. In other words lots of left-brain with a right-brain veneer.

In a similar way, people with "so called" uncreative jobs can challenge themselves to invent a whole new way of doing things. It's all about having a creative attitude rather than a creative job title.

Some people manage to fit in two jobs, to honor the requirements of both sides of the brain. Fay Weldon (heroine) got up early to write her novels before heading off to work in an advertising agency. T.S. Elliot got up early to write his epic poems before heading off to work as a lawyer. (How extreme is this polarity – the rigid, rule based world of law and the fluid, mystical world of poetry!)

If we take away all the expectations we have around work, it becomes much easier to "just do it." Our problems arrive when we need the job to make us happy or make us feel valued, important or indispensible.

And were did this pattern begin?

If we need external validation from a job, it's often a reflection of the fact that we needed validation and approval from Dad... and we didn't get it. There are thousands of Hollywood movies built on the premise that "Dad didn't give me enough time and attention." These vary between the poignant and the sentimental, but the truth is, each generation changes the game of parenting – that's how the species evolves. Many of us had fathers who were always at work and/or were challenged in the emotional intelligence department. Many men were fathers before emotional intelligence was even invented!

It's time to let go of the story that Dad didn't give us enough attention "on purpose!" - he either didn't have it to give or didn't know how to give it.

The wonderful thing about the realm of energy is that everything is fluid. If something is lacking in the relationship between two people, then either person can contribute to what's missing – it's only pride, and the need to be right, that stops us doing this.

"But it's too late!"

In the realm of energy there is no time. This is what is so brilliant about the metaphysical world. It means we can fix problems from the past in the present moment.

The alternative of course is to fix things in the physical world, where time does exist. This is clearly ineffective. The incident isn't in present time (duh!) so how are we going to find the place we need to get back to? Even the Tardis is unreliable. Going back to the past to fix our problems is also expensive and time consuming. Psychotherapy doesn't come cheap and emotional pain has a long tail.

So, we need to reverse our perception and make our contribution to the missing energy.

"Dad didn't give me time/validation/approval"... becomes "I didn't give Dad time/validation/approval."

It's more accurate. For skeptics who might say, "How can a small child give validation to an adult?" we must remember that it's only our body that's infantile - our spirit is much older than this. And between these two is our mind, which as we have seen, is not so innocent! If we could honestly remember our childhood, we might recall some of its more judgmental thoughts...

Of course, we hide these thoughts in our subconscious mind. But we feel guilty for having them, so we relieve the guilt by creating punishments.

1. Self-punishment Strategy No. 1 "I'll make sure I'm always broke. I'll show the world that Dad didn't give me what I needed to grow up - by remaining a child! There's no clearer way to demonstrate my stunted growth, than being unable to provide for myself financially."

2. Self-punishment Strategy No. 2. "Because I don't know how to turn off the energy of the story 'my Dad didn't appreciate me' it has to attach itself to a new authority person. This practically ensures that I will always end up working for a boss who doesn't appreciate me." (And in Chloe's case a landlord who doesn't listen.)

Hmmmm. Chloe scores a double whammy in the left-brain chair. It's time to break the pattern and change the never-ending story.

We do this by venturing into the desert so that we can find Dad and let him off the hook. We forgive him for disappointing us. It doesn't matter if he's dead - he's still around somewhere in energetic form. We apologize for attacking him with the guilt trip of our hard luck story. We show him how successful we are after all – or how successful we are about to become. We say sorry. We feel his relief. We turn off the energy of Dad didn't appreciate me, didn't love me, didn't listen. We turn off the energy of "the world is a hard, cruel place full of snipers and snakes". We say sorry again for putting him through this shit. We feel his laughter. We feel his blessing. We get him out of the desert and bring him home to the center. That's it - end of story. It can be that quick, that easy, and that joyful.

Chloe feels inspired to start a new round of job-hunting; now that she is optimistic about a different outcome. She remembers the old work story in a different light. When she does a rough calculation on the amount of time she spent just *thinking* about her boss and the clients and resisting the dreaded spreadsheets, she realizes she could have written a novel or two already! So much can happen in the gaps of life once we release all the energy we expend on our spinning wheels.

She still needs a new perspective on her ex boyfriend, but this requires the right-brain side of the equation and as it's getting late, this will have to wait until tomorrow. In the same way that trapped energy affects our work life, trapped energy also affects our relationships.

On the other hand Simon Cowell does live in the world of form so Chloe is getting up super early to hit the gym. The combination of spiritual clarity and upper arm definition should cover all the bases.

Stop, step away from the desert, there's nothing to see here

DAY TWENTY

In between the desert and the deep blue sea

Incredibly I have reached the half way mark of forty days and forty nights. It is appropriate to be at mid point on the day that Chloe does the right-brain exercise. The portal to the right-brain is an exciting place where most of us like to camp. We sit in our ramshackle tents with all our friends waiting for the box office to open, eagerly anticipating the forthcoming event. We talk about it a lot. We think about how it will be. There is much camaraderie outside the pearly gateway to the right-brain.

We instinctively know that this is what we are here for. On the other side is our destiny - our purpose in life, the awareness of which will change everything. We will suddenly know the answers to our most heartfelt questions. *"Why am I here? What's my purpose in all this? Where is my true love? When am I going to be rich and famous?"* (Ok the last one isn't so heartfelt but in our attempt to make more of the unconscious conscious let's put it in there.)

At this point in the proceedings, the source of all creativity is laughing and wondering why we don't just get out of the sleeping bag and open the gate. If the source of all creativity used such a primitive form of communication as words, the words would probably be "The gate isn't locked." (We would add 'duh!' on the end of that sentence but the source of all creativity is supreme love, which contains no trace of sarcasm, judgment or frustration of any kind.)

If we are going to take part in a collective paradigm shift of creativity we really, really need to know why we are so afraid of crossing the threshold.

Self-help adage No. 20 **Let go of your mother**

In the realm of the right-brain things are very different. To enter, we have to leave behind the left-brain system of rules, logic and five sensory perceptions. This is slightly worrying, but we are determined to carry on regardless. We've read enough self-help books now; we want to experience the damn thing. If it's too strange, we can always come back again to the safety of the other side. This is when, like a political party fighting for re-election, the left-brain will turn up the volume and turn on the spin. It sounds something like...

"This will be like a bad acid trip that you can't stop."

"You like it here, you know the rules."

"Who are you now Alice in Wonderland? this stuff is for kids and mad Queens."

We know that our relationship with the masculine life force is a big factor in determining what we *do* in the world. When this plays out at the physical level, it is usually represented by a job of some kind. If we have an overactive left-brain, we love the status and mental stimulation of a career.

If we make a move towards the right-brain we become drawn to a different dimension. We want a form of self-expression that benefits the whole rather than the individual. We want to feel connected, to feel something greater than adrenaline. So if the masculine energy is about what we are "doing" in the world, what is the feminine energy about?

It's all about "being."

In the quantum world everything is connected. In other words everything is in relationship with everything else. Nothing exists separately; it exists by the way it relates to its surroundings. To thrive at this level, it is very important that we learn "how to be" - in relationship. We learn the mechanics of how to relate to others, from our very first relationship. Unless we emerged into the world from the titanium pod of some visiting spaceship, this relationship is with our mother.

If we could remember what it was like to be a baby we would probably recall an experience of oneness. I remember my own children, before they absorbed the rules of perception operating on this planet. They would gaze at their fingers; seemingly unaware that this was a hand that "belonged" to them. They heard strange sounds that meant nothing at all and would observe shapes that appeared over the pram, no doubt presuming these also, were soon to be discovered parts of their own nature.

There was no "self" no identity. There was just "being." Just hanging out with all that is. If this sounds boring, don't forget that the energy behind "all that is" is love. So this could be described as a state of "Being in love" which adds a whole other dimension to the experience.

Gradually, like a visitor adapting to new surroundings, the five sensory perceptual system downloads into the baby...

Sight: I can see shapes that have some sort of form. They are not me!

Sound: I can hear, though it will be a while before I get to grips with language.

Touch: Now I know what those hands are for.

Smell: This is the easiest as it requires no interpretation.

Taste: I know this will be important one day but for now I'll use it as a way to understand and will put everything in my mouth.

Gradually we leave the realm of "being" and enter the world of "thinking about being." Our first thoughts are probably fear based – *"If I am separate from all that is, how will I get my needs met?"* Thoughts call forth the need for a strategy - now our left-brain is really firing up. *"In order to survive in this new place, I need to attach myself to something."*

Years later when we wake up and find ourselves camped outside the Gates of Supreme Creativity; we realize we are slightly diminished versions of our former selves. In our attempts to feel safe, we have left parts of our spirit attached to the earthing rods of other people. Our first reaction is to get some coffee, light a fire and sing about the glory days of "being in love" but it's more effective to start heading back to the original scene of the crime...

Neediness... the not so grassy knoll

Let's go back to the baby and try to imagine our earliest thoughts...

Bliss, bliss, bliss, bliss... Oh my God where am I? Who is this woman? Why doesn't she realize what I want? I've been sending out really clear signals. She doesn't understand energetic communication. I'm in serious trouble. Perhaps she doesn't love me.

The scene of the crime is a perception... If she doesn't love me, how will I get my needs met?

As fully functioning adults we can say, "of course we love the baby - this is crazy" but we forget one thing. The baby reads the energy of the whole mother, not just the conscious bit. Other parts of the mother are feeling overwhelmed by giving birth, frightened they aren't doing it right, anxious about money, guilty about going back to work etc. The baby absorbs all this new data energetically.

Also, the baby comes from the source of supreme love. On earth we have a diluted form of conditional love. Being an energetic communicator the baby picks up on this strange new atmosphere straight away. Things would be so different if it arrived kitted out with a *Star Trek* backpack that facilitated breathing in any atmosphere but the source of creativity likes to play with raised stakes and reckons we're smart enough to figure things out.

Just so we're clear of the difference, this is what supreme love sounds like...

I love you.

This is what earthly love sounds like...

I love you - as long as you love me back, make me feel special, turn up on time, understand when I'm late, dislike the people I dislike, like the people I like (but not so much that you end up sleeping with them), show me affection when I'm feeling needy, keep your distance when I'm feeling independent and know the difference between the two without me having to tell you...

Can you imagine entering a world where supreme love (aka oxygen) is scarce, while being in the body of an infant? No wonder we lose our awareness of ourselves as a creative force.

The exercise for today is to feel comfortable with neediness. Chloe has to imagine that her knight is never coming. That she is in a place where he cannot hear her no matter how witty her stories. He cannot see her no matter how cellulite free her thighs. She cannot reach him, touch him, hold him, be held by him.

Though she has projected this scenario onto Simon, she realizes it is a replay of a much earlier experience with her mother. She leans further into the feelings so she can fully experience them.

"This is what it must feel like to be a junkie" she groans.

"I know - hideous isn't it? Just stick with it".

Eventually her grimace softens and her body relaxes. She's stopped fighting and come to a level of acceptance around the helplessness.

A few minutes later she smiles. She has surrendered into the heart of a strange paradox.

She is powerless...and at peace.

The deep blue sea... scary but better than the desert!

HALF-WAY NOTES

DAY TWENTY ONE

What other significant events mark this halfway point? It will soon be Halloween. There is the smell of gunpowder in the air and a feeling of endings and beginnings. Chloe is moving out in a few days so she's starting to pack her stuff. But most significant of all, tomorrow she is meeting up with Simon Cowell! His window is open.

Chloe is trying not to have expectations but in Buddhist terms we know this is a bit of a problem. "Trying" creates energy. We used to think this was a good thing, and we are over familiar with phrases that involve "trying." Our school reports were littered with "must try harder." Our parents were raised on 'If at first you don't succeed, try, try again'. At first glance, it seems a good attribute to be strong-minded, but in many cases this is just strong left-minded. And in a few cases it is even strong bloody-minded.

When we look back through history we remember the people who have made great breakthroughs by not giving up - scientists, explorers, inventors. We forget the stories of people who used the same principle to poor effect (soldiers in trenches, trained in hand to hand combat mowed down by machine guns). "Keep trying, the sacrifice is worth it, if we're strong minded enough we can win."

We also forget that the people known for their relentless efforts (Edison when he invented the light bulb, Newton when he discovered gravity) achieved breakthrough when they gave up trying and opened themselves up to inspiration from the other side.

In the quantum world "trying" is not such a highly sought after strategy. When Luke Skywalker failed to levitate his space ship out of the mud saying, "I tried" his little mentor says "That's why you fail. There is no try. Do." We love "trying" because it is performed by the mind, something we can control. "Inspired doing" requires us to give up control. This is a conundrum, because the less we feel in control of our life, the more liable we are to get angry.

Another important aspect of the quantum world, is that it's not "how" we try but "why" we try that drives the outcome...

Thoughts like "Because I really, really need this" are driven by an energy of lack, which creates more lack. Thoughts like "Because if I don't get this thing I'm going to be so disappointed' are driven by an energy of fear, which creates more fear. We have to change these thoughts before we go any further.

Self-help adage No. 21 What you resist persists

Here's the tricky thing about energy. It's neutral - like electricity. The ability to make toast - good. The possibility of dying when you put your knife in to extract it – bad. The source of supreme creativity cannot interpret our preferences as good or bad, it just gives us an endless supply of whatever voltage we are currently running on. There is a fundamental communication problem between the physical and the metaphysical world. The source of supreme creativity doesn't understand our primitive language, it just reads our vibration. Miscommunications abound, a bit like the mother with the baby. Whatever we are vibrating, we are given more of.

Imagine the scene. We are sitting, minding our own business, feeling sorry for ourselves. Though we *seem* to be doing nothing, we are in fact vibrating (we can't not vibrate because deep down, we are energetic beings of moving molecules.) The source of supreme creativity, to which we are linked, reads our vibration and responds accordingly.

Source of Supreme Creativity: "Ah! You seem to like that, let me give you some more."

Us: 'No, no. I just picked it up for a second. It was lying on the nursery floor and I wondered what it was. It seems to be a thought process called "extreme self loathing and hopeless despair". It's somebody else's. I didn't read the label. Stop!"

Source of Supreme Creativity: What are those strange noises you are making! They must be your way of saying thank you. What's that in your energy system now? I'm picking up anger, frustration and intense neediness.... hey let me help you out with that."

Annoying isn't it, this communication thing. There is so much help available but we're tuned to the wrong channel. If we want help getting the things we want, we have to change our energy. We have to stop vibrating at a frequency of "Lack" and "Fear" and start vibrating at a frequency of "Love" and "Abundance."

So, that's easy then.

Chloe has stopped "trying" to let go of Simon (while desperately needing him to come back). She's letting go of him. In other words she is picturing him not coming back and being completely happy about it. There – that's the "Lack" dealt with. In fact she doesn't care if he comes back or not.

Oh no! This isn't letting go - it's throwing away! This isn't an act of love - it's a tantrum. If we're scared of losing the things we love, we trash them. We're back in the nursery. "I didn't like the blue truck anyway, it's rubbish, and the wheels don't even turn properly." Underneath this strategy is the fear of loss. We throw things away before they can mean very much to us. We know that if we are really honest about how valuable they are, then we find out we can't actually have them, we might die.

Not so easy then.

We need some wisdom from the chair. We need to go back to the original tantrum. This is with our mother. Having come from the source of supreme love, we attached ourselves and tried to get this energy from her. We had an expectation. We wanted a Goddess in earthly form. She failed to deliver. Rather than being understanding, like little emperors we became very angry. Then we closed the door.

It is our mother who stands in front of the portal to our creativity and we certainly haven't forgiven her. We act cool and nonchalant. We say we don't want to come in anyway. We're doing fine out here, having constructed our own little world where we rule. We put two fingers up to the source of supreme creativity, and go back to our bohemian life, congratulating ourselves on our ability to be independent and enigmatically creative. We wear the clothes, adopt the opinions and speak the lingo. Our image and vocabulary become a testament to the world of just how creative we are. We don't need anybody. From now on nobody will tell us what to do, nobody will disappoint us, nobody will let us down. We are warriors who are scared of nothing (well, apart from our feelings.)

You have to admit it all looks really good. The downside is, on a bad day it feels a bit rubbish. On a good day it feels like nothing much at all. Because ironically, the mechanism that allows us to feel things is on the other side of the door. Time to apologize to our mothers, give up the tantrum and come home.

As Chloe sits in the chair she tries to imagine what balance would feel like – on one side there is the "trying to get" and on the other side there is the "throwing away." She holds the energy of "trying to get" in her right hand and the energy of "throwing away" in her left. Then she slowly brings her hands together. A new energy starts to emerge from her clasped hands. It feels innocent and playful, like an urchin child that Chloe recognizes as herself. Then she visualizes a re-union between this unruly child and her mother.

The tantrum of "throwing away" and the manipulation of "trying to get" fade away and are replaced by a sense of gratitude towards her mother and an appreciation for being here. Now Chloe doesn't want to leave the chair!

But that's enough for today. She has a hot date for tomorrow and a dilemma of a different kind - to keep the remains of her tan or to exfoliate it down the plughole. Does she want her skin to look good or feel good? She figures that by the time her clothes start coming off the lights will be out, so the tan will go unnoticed. As she slowly climbs the stairs, she realizes that she has already decided to sleep with him.

I can't stand it!

DAY TWENTY TWO

Chloe did not return so hopefully she had a great evening. Of course she had a great evening, that was never in doubt. How she manages the morning that follows the evening is the test. That's when the neediness comes. But she knows how to survive in the storm. She may even be able to fly through it.

Self-help adage No. 22 **All you need is trust... and a little bit of pixie dust**

Simon Cowell is in the music business, something I know a little bit about. Chloe was level headed when they met. Understandably, after four years with Jack Sparrow she was rather cautious. She didn't want another volatile relationship. He, on the other hand, was very keen... "At last an independent woman who's happy with 'no strings' sex." They realized they had a million things in common. After a few months of bonding, Chloe found that she had fallen hopelessly in love with him. She made the mistake of sharing this revelation. Simon immediately backed off and announced that they should be "just good friends."

This is a fairly typical Mexican stand off whereby two people, both "in control" on the surface and both "needy" below the surface, get into a relationship and attempt a merger. At first everything is great, the surface molecules agree on how wonderful they both are. After a while however, as bonding increases, hoards of needy molecules emerge from their jails shouting, "Free at last! Free at last! Thank God Almighty Free at last!" They cross the border creating mayhem, drinking tequila and crying about how hard things have been.

The merged "in control" molecules of both Chloe and Simon try to push them back, but the gate is now open and the swarm begins. The "in control" molecules hold hands and run for the hills. Some of them (the more feminine ones who were no doubt wearing inappropriate shoes) trip and fall. The others (more masculine and focused) escape and build a cool hangout on the moral high ground. Chloe and Simon's merged molecules now survey the landscape of their new home. Most of Simon's molecules are up in the hills. Most of Chloe's are in the refugee camp below, desperately trying to distance themselves from the prison break molecules of neediness but inevitably succumbing to the status quo of handouts and despair.

It's winner takes all in the mergers and acquisitions business. In the merger of their shared relationship, Simon became CEO of the new business and Chloe was left managing the less desirable molecules. From an energetic point of view, relationships are tricky, leading many people (like Simon) to think they are best avoided. Physically we can live without any close relationships (particularly now we have technology) but "Cool on the hill" can soon turn into "Fool on the hill." Spiritually, we don't want to live with a few elite molecules. Spiritually we are holistic – this means no marginalizing the molecules!

The blueprint for "falling in love" is developed in childhood. After separating from the source of supreme love, we enter adulthood with a sense that something is missing. Traditionally, girls look for its replacement in the form of romantic love - if mother failed as replacement deity, perhaps a man could do better! (Girls are clearly not known for their powers of reasoning.) Boys on the other hand tend to look for its replacement in the form of a career. (If I'm really successful *everyone* will love me.)

The music business is an extreme example of this, as it incorporates both fame and celebrity. It's like a mini galaxy. There are a few stars, who get a glimpse of "who they really are." They create (that's what you do when you know who you are). Around each star is an orbiting ring of business people who are special - because they are close to the star. Further out in space there are the fans who are not so special... but who gain status either by their in depth knowledge of the star or because they have a "friend" in the inner circle.

It's all a recipe to make everyone very insecure. The star is worried in case he can't keep creating and often feels fraudulent and not a "proper" star. The inner circle are scared of losing momentum and falling into the outer hemisphere where they'll lose all specialness along with most of their friends. They have to keep spinning like crazy. The fans criticize the inner circle for hogging the light and heat and try to knock them out of their orbit.

The star gets worried about burn out and creates a barrier made from strange eccentricities. He/she will not perform unless a list of requirements are adhered to - the stage has to be shaped like a dolphin, all green sweets have to be removed from the dressing room, the follow spot operator has to be Russian. The inner circle love these rules as it gives them something special to do, and because rules bring a bit of left-brain sanity to a slightly unreal world.

The music business, like all other businesses, has evolved to allow women into its midst, but it is still a bit of a boy's club where people hate to grow up. Basically, Peter Pan type figures get to hang out with a bunch of lost boys and play pirates all day. When women were allowed to join, their choice of roles was limited to Wendy or Tinkerbell. The "Wendy's" became long suffering secretaries or long suffering wives. They darned socks, booked flights, smoothed ruffled egos and cleared up the mess created by all those skirmishes. They never joined the heat and excitement of the battle but looked on from the sidelines and always had one of those oversize bags containing paracetamol, mobile phone chargers and spare swords.

"Tinkerbells" were pretty special as they were allowed out with the boys. They got to have lots of fun during the day, but at night when Peter went home to Wendy, there was a lot of sitting outside the tree house sulking. Though they were jealous of the "special relationship" between Peter and Wendy, they convinced themselves they had a much better deal. After all, day was better than night - it was longer. Until the night came, bringing darkness, lack of belief and sobbing. Tinkerbells existed on crumbs... which is, after all, an appropriate food source for a fairy.

Chloe crossed a line.

She met Simon Cowell as Tinkerbell, but pretty soon she wanted to be his Wendy. This is very bad timing. Simon is in the middle of a horrible divorce and was looking for respite in the form of "best friends who have sex... and no commitment." This brings us back to the energy, and how it is lining up in the various energy centers of the body - specifically the second chakra where all the sexual energy vibrates; the fourth where the heart is looking for connection; and the sixth where the mind is desperately trying to carry off the "brilliant career" strategy.

Because men have a long association with the Knight archetype, they wear metal breastplates over their heart (fourth center of energy.)

Vulnerability is not an option when there are so many battles to fight and damsels to rescue. Meanwhile the sexual energy below and the mental energy above operate quite well independently, resulting in conquests in both bedroom and boardroom. (Note conquests not collaborations.) Men have developed a "by pass" that would be the envy of any town planner.

Women on the other hand tend to keep their heart open. If they didn't, their children would die and there would be no next generation... leading inevitably to the end of the story of evolution on this planet. This makes it slightly tricky when it comes to the sex part. Once the energy in their second chakra starts to vibrate, their heart starts vibrating as well, creating an association, which looks and feels pretty much like love.

Of course the real mastery in all this would be to line up all of the energy centers and create a super highway, from the second, through the fourth and sixth, out through the crown of the head to the source of supreme love and back down again. If this happened, sex would not be limited to a below the waist experience but would be a super cosmic tantric one. In order to do this of course, all the gunk and bad energy would need to be excavated and recycled first, but if we're waiting for an incentive, they don't come much bigger than this.

Chloe has made huge progress in her attempts to restore her environment. We can only wait to see what kind of effect this has had on Simon Cowell.

The eternal triangle

DAY TWENTY THREE

My house is a hive of activity. My daughters are home for the weekend bringing hilarious tales of college life. Over breakfast they outbid each other with stories of drunken housemates, eccentric teachers and boys they'd like to kiss. Chloe arrives with news from the dating front line. There are now three generations of women in my kitchen and enough animation for a Disney cartoon.

Simon Cowell is impressed with the new internally remodeled Chloe. He seeks her advice on his work, his divorce and his crazy ex wife. Chloe has now joined the "beyond craziness" club, so is a bit of an expert. She is wise, sexy and sympathetic (an impressive hat trick of archetypes – Sage, Femme fatale and Nurse). Though she has survived her descent to the underworld and calmed the Damsel, she is anxious to distance herself from the particular brand of craziness favored by Simon's ex wife. She listens in horror to a Heather Mills McCartney storyline of injustice and psychotic rage. Simon Cowell's ex wife doesn't have a damsel in her dungeon, she has a wicked witch.

Self-help adage No. 23 Everything will be ok as soon as you are ok with everything

Back to the quantum world of energy. If we are scared of certain molecules and seal them up in silos and concrete bunkers, they don't go away. The half-life of an emotion goes on for a very long time. On a global scale, we are now dealing with the repercussions of this strategy. We have huge numbers of people who get to play out the Damsel part – refugees, homeless, unemployed, single mothers, redundant fathers. We have a smaller number of people who get to play the Wicked Witch part. Both the ones outside the system (terrorists, tribal warlords, thieves) and the ones within the system (Bad bosses, corrupt politicians, unethical bankers).

In the holistic world, there is a price to pay for our strategy of distancing ourselves from the things we don't like. What we resist gets a whole lot bigger, just at a time when the world got a whole lot smaller. One country's pollution becomes another country's acid rain. One corporation's brand expansion shrinks another nation's cultural richness. One mother's golden child gets blown up by another mother's damaged one. The Internet has upped the stakes. It has made the bad guys more visible. We are now angry at discovering the hidden agendas of the villains within the system (in commerce and government). But we are also frightened of the terrorists outside the system. (We know the statistics are small but the visual images are wide screen and high definition).

If we are frightened, our anger becomes impotent instead of useful. Anger can serve as an early warning sign that truth has been violated. It can be used as fuel for personal change, social change and the correcting of injustice. In our quest to be "civilized" and to have things "look nice" we have forgotten the positive power of anger. Because we have shadow figures of the Wicked Witch and the Bad Queen, we distance ourselves from our anger and pretend to be Snow White. "Of course I *would* do something about it but it's all so hopeless. There's no-one to back me up, people are trying to kill me and I have these seven small people to support."

This brings us to the real crux of creativity - namely the shadows that are created by all that light. If we want to gain access to the right side of the brain, where the energy is chaotic and uncontrollable, we have to face the dark side of the feminine - destruction. In this world of duality, there has to be a flip side of creative power. We can't be naïve and pray for more creativity without understanding what that means. We can't summon it to do our bidding, and then make it hide away again, like the genie in Aladdin's lamp.

We have to build our capacity to stand in this energy without being blown to bits. The only way we can do this is to become benign ourselves, by excavating our hidden agendas – after all, these agendas aren't quite so hidden in the quantum world. First we need to give up the charade that we are Snow White and admit the fact that we have needs – at least seven of them, and we have bad thoughts - particularly when we look in the mirror ('It's not fair! She's prettier! Other people are getting all the attention! I want to kill someone!)

Once we own up to these parts of our mind, we need to sit in the chair with them and tell them in a kind but firm way that it's time to grow up now. This is what it takes to re-parent ourselves. The plan for the next stage of evolution, whereby we increase our consciousness and become powerfully creative goes something like this...

We are born. We feel a sense of lack and powerlessness. The world is in trouble and requires us to become brilliantly creative. We look to our parents to provide for all our needs, and to manage our emotions for us. They don't. We go looking for help in the external world.

We realize we are the help.

We learn to meet our own needs and manage our own anger.

We make some clear choices about what to do next.

Of course at the moment our collective story is stuck around "we go looking for help in the external world" and far from moving on to the next chapter, we are absorbed in the sub plot of blame. We spend a lot of time moaning about our lack of power to change the system. Meanwhile our anger gets used up in judging all the shadow figures we have collectively created. The media whips up our judgment into whirlwinds of indignation that seem to blow over after a couple of days.

Whirlwinds are useless. What we want is a perfect storm! We want to walk into the eye of the storm and start directing. Becoming a storm director comes later. For now, the following steps (for the mind, heart and body) are enough.

1. Mind: Be aware of the inner Wicked Witch so that it is less likely to be projected out into the world.
2. Heart: Become more balanced – we do this by having the courage and accountability to meet our own needs and manage our own anger.
3. Body: Make a choice to do something – hopefully now it will be a more conscious, creative one.

A word about choice...

We make the mistake of thinking that "directing in the storm" is about making "clear" choices – in other words well articulated requests. Management consultants spend hours cleaning up the wording and terminology of mission statements, as if greater eloquence is all that is needed to send the business off in a better direction. New agers think that if we become more precise in the wording of our personal prayers we would have a greater chance of manifesting our goals. But this is all "head" stuff. It's the clarity of our inner channels – our whole system - that's important.

When our inner channels are clear, we are less likely to vibrate at the level of neediness and anger. When we change our vibration, we change our point of attraction.

Meanwhile my kitchen is buzzing. Chloe has had an idea for a TV drama. She and my daughters are discussing heroines, while eating toast and peanut butter. Something has changed. Chloe is not analyzing every detail of the evening before. She is not checking her blackberry for messages or fantasizing about Simon's plans for the future. Her mind is in the present moment, comfortable with whatever activity the source of supreme creativity wants to direct her towards.

Meanwhile, Simon is back in his office managing the drama of other peoples' lives. He loves creativity, but he likes a creative force he can control. His world is full of "to do" lists, demanding clients, important meetings and stressful deadlines. It looks cool. But though he doesn't admit it, he often feels dead inside. He likes to read about being in the flow but he's scared about the balancing part. He knows that leaning too far to the right will bring up those shadowy figures... all it takes is a few degrees, and that doesn't mean a bunch of divas with a list of rider requirements.

When will I see you again? (You don't have to answer that)

DAY TWENTY FOUR

Not self-help adage No. 24 but immortal Bob Dylan
lyrics... "He not busy being born is busy dying."

I seem to have come to a complete full stop on *the Sextant*. The
distractions of normal life have taken over. France is a distant
memory. My insomnia is bad. I am well and truly in resistance.

The cairns of self-help books are not helping. This is something bigger
than the usual reluctance to hold the dynamic tension between the
written and the unwritten. The brilliant Steven Pressfield writes better
than anybody about this place of "resistance" and the rigorous discipline
needed to occupy its territory with focus and military determination. I
take his advice and show up in front of the laptop refusing to budge. I
see through the strategy of guerilla like distractions and the siege of the
blank screen. Still the words will not come.

As we have seen, one of the requirements of the world of duality is the
necessity to constantly check for balance. Even simple things like
walking, when slowed down, involve a shift from stability (two feet on
the ground) to instability (one foot off the ground) and back to stability.
A speeded up life means we can successfully avoid actually experiencing
the instability part. Like riding a bike, life is easier when you're going
fast. It certainly requires less skill at balancing.

The difficulty occurs when things slow down and we become more
conscious of them. This is a paradox - we want to become more fully
conscious so that we can appreciate life more, but this can lead us to
feel a little unstable along the way.

The urge of the unconscious is to reproduce itself. Unless we intervene
everything just becomes more of what it is already. We can see this in
nature – the landscape reproduces itself without our intervention. We

can see it in ourselves - our thoughts, beliefs and patterns reproduce themselves without our conscious awareness. We react to certain people and events in an automatic way.

If we want to be creative, we have to access new and different thoughts, not automatic ones. In order to do this we need to become more conscious. The urge of consciousness is not to reproduce itself but to know itself. This is a very big new chapter in our evolutionary history.

Over the past few hundred years we have become really good at controlling things. We have used our creativity to change the natural world. We have landscaped gardens, mined the earth for minerals, built bridges over water and tunneled through hard rock. We have split atoms. During the course of this we have created some huge problems – inequality, terrorism and pollution. These problems require more creativity than we currently have access to.

But the universe is one step ahead. The creativity we require is already waiting for us - if we expand our consciousness to encapsulate it. Maybe that's why I'm feeling so stretched. I'm giving birth to an entirely new part of myself. Some aspect of my unconsciousness that has never seen the light of day is trying to come through and make itself known. This is pretty inconvenient timing. I'm now trying to produce a book and a whole new part of my psyche simultaneously.

I should have seen the signs. One of my chief roles (Mother) collapsed when my last child left for college a couple of months ago. Rather than experiencing the empty nest, I "adopted" Chloe, who just happened to have a landlord problem and was temporarily homeless.

Just as nature has its seasons, all things have their time for being and ceasing to be. As Bob says, "if they're not busy being born, they're busy dying." The psyche has different templates through which it births the energy of the universe – these templates form our archetypes. Because the templates are in our psyche, they are with us for the whole of our lifetime, but at various stages they can play a leading role, a supporting role, or even have some time off. In my case, it's now time for "Mom" to leave the stage.

Now that we understand the value of holism, we know that the psyche craves full expression. Our unconscious longs to "know" itself. But our tendency as human beings is to resist this fuller "knowing." We become over familiar and confident with certain roles. They become a way that we define ourselves. If we really like the role and we are getting a lot of applause, the role can become our whole identity. This is a problem. It is only one aspect of ourselves but now it thinks it is us! It doesn't want to get off the stage! Like some ageing Hollywood star who imagines that (with a bit of surgery and an extra layer of make up) they can play a thirty year old, this can all get a bit sad.

In general, we are not very good at relinquishing the role of one archetype and holding the space for the new one to emerge. We are not good at "Holding space" in general. To us it is a contradiction in terms ... there is nothing to hold! Being comfortable with nothingness is another way to put it - being in a chair while not doing anything; not listening; not seeing; not thinking.

Just being.

Most of us can achieve this as long as we don't have to do the "not thinking" part. We can't meditate because we can't turn off the thinking. That's the part that won't leave the stage.

Many of the roles that men use to define themselves, being work orientated, don't have a biological imperative. As long as they are mental rather than physical, these roles can survive way past the usual retirement age. On the other hand, a woman who holds tenaciously to the role of Mother, or one who holds onto the role of Femme Fatale when they should be embracing the Wise Woman can look slightly unhinged. It just "looks all wrong." Society is her mirror on the wall.

Men on the other hand can play the Entrepreneur or the Don Juan into old age without looking out of place. Damage happens, but it happens on an internal level. If "what wants to emerge" is not given expression, the spirit can wither and die. In men, (because they can deny this inner process for much longer) this often happens quickly. They are literally blind-sided by the hit when it arrives. In women, it tends to play out slower.

A lot of illness is the manifestation of "unlived life." We tend to interpret this as "things I didn't do" instead of "things I didn't become." We can then blame life for not creating the right circumstances - like job opportunities or foreign travel. In reality, our disappointment about the "unlived life" is less about events that did not happen and more about our refusal to give expression to life's full diversity. Our attachment to certain roles, and our desire to control the process, blocks what wants to emerge.

Meanwhile I have to sit and develop a relationship with what is not yet here. It is a very strange thing to be pregnant with the unknown. We don't know if we'll be any good at the new thing. We don't believe it will come naturally. We're scared we'll be booed off stage at the first performance. We sit in the wings waiting. We have no visual imagery to reassure us. No sounds, other than our heartbeat and our breath. They are the two things that connect us to the source of supreme creativity. Not our thoughts. Our thoughts won't help us in this place... they will merely serve to drive us mad.

Birth is about giving up control and trusting the unknown.

Because it wants to meet itself.

Waiting for the idea to come

DAY TWENTY FIVE

Not self-help adage No. 25 but immortal Randy Newman lyrics... **"You gotta roll with the punches."**

I'm still in the labor ward trying to birth my creativity. This process is trickier than it seems - a bit like physical birth. When I was pregnant with my first child, I read a book about childbirth (being a bit left-brain, Amazon is my answer to most things.) Of course it was a complete waste of time. As soon as the contractions started I forgot everything I'd read. The intelligence was in my brain, but the process was happening in my body and the two didn't connect until after the baby was born.

Whilst it's easy to forgive ourselves when physical pain severs the connection to our higher intention (peaceful birth with soft music turns into maximum drugs and screaming) we tend to forget the difficulties of emotional pain. Creativity seems to walk hand in hand with emotional pain.

A surprising number of writers suffer from mood disorders so I am in good company. Charles Dickins, Virginia Woolf and Jimi Hendrix all suffered from manic depression. Creativity is a double-edged sword in more ways than one. We alternate between mania and depression. During the mania we can write prolifically, then we flip over into the depression of "writers block" where we are unable to write anything at all. It's interesting to note the correlation between mental illness and chosen career – a whopping 70% for writers, musicians, poets and painters; a mere 25% for all other fields.

There seems to be no universal method for dealing with the pain of creativity. Throughout history, individuals have tackled it in a variety of ways. Some chose drugs and alcohol. Creativity is high voltage energy, which many of us find hard to contain. In the short term, drugs and alcohol can calm the edginess we feel, allowing us to soldier on, but in the long term this strategy can have disastrous consequences.

This reminds me of learning to ski. My left-brain knew the mechanics of ski-ing, but my fear prohibited me from being able to do it. My ski instructor got me to drink a couple of shots of vodka and suddenly I was able to relax enough to allow the knowledge of how to ski to integrate into my body. Of course more than a couple of shots would have had the opposite effect. F. Scott Fitzgerald wrote brilliantly while under the influence of alcohol, but as soon as he became an alcoholic his writing went totally downhill. There is a thin line between ski-ing gracefully with the muse and ending up in a broken heap at the bottom of the slope.

The only successful strategy for all this is learning to balance. Learning to "Be" in balance. This means picking up speed on our processing skills. If we get the neurons of both sides to fire really quickly, balance will become easier. This balanced state would produce some very desirable outcomes. Intuitive thought without the chaos. Clarity of decision without the dithering.

To alleviate my pre-natal depression, I decide to bake a lemon drizzle cake. Walking around the shops while in a semi creative haze is a slightly unnerving experience. I have completely forgotten what ingredients I need to buy. It is Halloween and the supermarket is full of bright displays in orange and black. There are cascades of themed sweets and cakes iced with skulls and bleeding fingers. I am now submerged in nostalgia, remembering all the Halloween parties arranged for trick or treat children.

Letting go of the Mother role happens in stages - particularly when you have made it into an art form. I remember the hours spent sewing elaborate costumes, the intricate carving of pumpkins – why have a roughly hewn smiley face when you can bask in the glory of a witch on a broomstick. I wonder how the next chapter of my life will materialize. Who will I be? I stand amidst the vegetables staring at the sea of orange orbs until a young sales assistant asks if he can help me with anything. *Yes actually, I'm looking for a part of my psyche.*

It's all so compulsive this nostalgia for the past. If I'm honest I didn't really enjoy things as much I think I did. Like the stickers on the rear view mirrors of cars, the past should have a label "Warning things in the imagination are more real than they appear." It's because we love the feeling involved in nostalgia. We forget the stress but remember the momentary glow. If we understand this we can consciously apply it to the present moment and change the ratio. Glow more. Stress less.

Experience more. Think less.

I give up on shopping. The problem with a collapsing role is that what is underneath the role gets revealed in all its glory – the sense of lack that underpins the role. It is the need for self-esteem through the eyes of others that creates the perfect pumpkins.

Outside the supermarket, a gaggle of girls stand at the bus stop, dressed to the nines. There is a sexy witch with a huge hat and tiny skirt; a fairy with clinging sparkly leotard and wings; a vamp with plunging neckline emphasized by a trail of fake blood. This is how the unconscious speaks - via an excuse. It says, "This is not me... Halloween demands that I dress up."

Of course the boys dress up too, but they can wear an old sheet or some bandages. Dressing up for them is a lark. Dressing up for the girls is an excuse to express their unconscious desires. They can cavort as sexy minxes and then deny all responsibility for an aspect of their sexuality that they don't want to own.

It's difficult to see who has the short straw in the boys versus girls debate. The girls struggle with the mirror that society holds up for them. They have to be sexy to get the boy, innocent when they've got the boy (don't make him jealous of other boys), nurturing when they've got the baby, then back to sexy again (don't make Dad jealous of the baby.) It's a difficult and exhausting one-woman play to pull off.

The boys always had it easier - get the girl, get a job. But now things are becoming more difficult for them too. They have to be alpha male to get the girl, funny to keep the girl (the macho stuff wears thin), new caring male when the baby comes along, while remaining alpha male in order to get laid occasionally. The girls smile and say, "Welcome to my world" or something equally unhelpful.

This whole "roles" thing that the ego has created is very flawed and in need of a complete overhaul. If we stopped using roles to create our identity then it would be a lot easier to give them up when their time is over. We fall in love with our roles. Like Narcissus by the side of the pool, we fall in love with the identities we have created. We fear that if we let them go, there will be no reflection in the mirror... we will cease to be.

A shiver runs down my spine that has nothing to do with Halloween. I need a ritual. I get home, light a candle and sit in the chair. Like a solo occupant of a movie theatre, I watch the flickering light and summon up images to project onto the blank magnolia wall. I think of my children and re-live as many moments as I can possibly conjure up. Hours pass. As each scene passes I bless it and move onto the next one. At times I laugh and at others cry, but then I always cry at the best movies. Then the screen goes blank and I take a deep breath. As the credits roll, I imagine myself letting go of all the memories.

Letting go means releasing the good and the bad. Of course we're scared that the good might not come again but we can't feel yesterday's joy today. The most we can hope for is vague nostalgia. Poignancy is evocative, but it's not joy. Joy is only available in the present moment. The present moment is exclusive. It can't share itself with the past or the future. If it is untainted, it is the perfect canvas for the source of supreme creativity to engage with. If we can just keep away the delusions of thoughts long enough, we can be impregnated with something far more divine.

I sit in the dark and wait.

Darkness visible

DAY TWENTY SIX

Cold sunny day. Still no words on the laptop screen, but I feel optimistic. My friend Penny emailed details of a mask-making workshop that is taking place tomorrow. She had booked, but is now unable to attend so asked if I wanted her place. Given that I am contemplating the nature of identity and roles, and I have no plans for the next few days, this seems perfect serendipity.

Self-help adage No. 26 Breathe

I decide to go for a long walk in the park ("Walking with intent" is a feature of many self-help books). I'm not sure whether I believe this. I've walked miles without inspiration of any kind. It's a frustrating fact that self-help theories can never be disputed. If they don't work then there must be something wrong with the clarity of intention not the methodology. Clarity of intention is a tricky thing to get right when we don't have access to our unconscious mind. I wonder how the girls outside the supermarket feel after their Halloween party. As they sit on the school bus, they may be absolutely clear about their intention to pass their end of year exams. Unfortunately, they also have to convince all the other girls – the ones in their head - some of whom are voting to have sex in a cat woman outfit.

I hope the mask workshop has some clues about how to pull together all the various aspects of my identity into one integrated whole. That would certainly create some clarity of intention. Meanwhile I am enjoying nature in the present moment. Autumn is perfect weather for walking. The trees are colorful; the fallen leaves are crunchy underfoot. I take deep breaths. They say breathing is the closest we come to receiving from the universe. We do it naturally... connecting to the "all that is." I once heard a chilling account of the ease with which children are kidnapped. Fear causes them to hold their breath. When we stop breathing we become static, rigid, silent and easy to pick up. Lifting a shouting, wriggling child who is having a tantrum is very difficult, as many mothers will attest. It's ironic that we instill fear as a cautionary measure... yet it makes us more unsafe.

What could we achieve in life if we weren't frightened? Our spirit isn't frightened of anything, but then again it knows it can't die, so thinks fear is over rated. It would be a shame if we got to the end of a very safe life of television watching, only to find that we had to repeat the same level all over again. Our spirit wants to evolve and play at higher levels, our mind disagrees and our hearts are torn. Which is why we have such a disconnect between body mind and spirit. The statistics of bad things happening is out of proportion to our fear level. There is also an argument to suggest that our fears are increasing the risks of bad things happening, rather than decreasing them. After all thoughts are energy, and energy becomes form.

I lean on a tree and watch an assortment of things in the air. Birds, kites and a model aeroplane controlled by a serious looking man with beard and oilskin jacket. The kids throw their kites in the air and run like crazy. They turn around and watch as the kite soars, holding tightly to the string. The whole scene is an homage to letting go. It strikes me the way we like to let go and hold on at the same time. We love to watch things fly as long as we can control them, as long as we can maintain ownership. "Look at my fabulous kite, my successful husband, my enchanting child."

Sadly, if we want to appreciate things forever, we have to cut the strings. No living thing thrives in captivity. If we had a sense of how connected everything is, we could sit in a field and watch numerous kites, we could walk through our life and interact with numerous people, the way nature lovers watch birds, without any requirement for ownership. It's a big ask and one that requires us to expand our hearts and alter our perception. The reason we want to own things is because we don't trust that they'll still be there tomorrow.

Our spirit thinks ownership is over rated. But then again if you own the universe, you're not going to obsess about a bit of dust. It would be just another thing you'd breathe life into.

I've got a clearer idea of what I'm going to write about now in the next chapter of my book. It's another dial for the sextant - *Fusion versus Connection*. This concept involves yet another confidence trick of the ego (just how many of them are there?!) The ego takes something good (connection to everybody) and turns it into something counterfeit (fusion to a small number of people.) When we become fused to people, we are not sure where we end and they begin. Our partner has a bad day... we are miserable. Our child loses a favorite toy... we become exasperated. Their emotional pain becomes our own. This doesn't help anybody. The spouse wants love, not the collusion of joint misery. The child wants to feel supported, not made to feel guilty. Children have highly tuned radar for emotional vibrations. If they detect that their mood determines their parents' wellbeing, they feel pressure. Obviously if everybody's upset, they feel really guilty. Being the center of the universe has its drawbacks – children believe that everything that goes wrong is "all their fault."

Most of us are fused to the people we love on some level. Because we have buried our emotional pain, we feel uncomfortable with the pain others are experiencing - if they come too close, it causes our undigested emotions to start vibrating. While we can keep most colleagues and friends at a safe enough distance, the people we are close to are always stumbling into the trip wire that sets us off. But what would it take for us to be in a state of non-resistance to whatever is going on? What would it be like if we could be with an upset partner or an angry child without reacting to the situation?

Of course the ego twists this 'not reacting" into dissociation and advises a strategy of disconnection. We put false barriers up because we don't believe we have any natural boundaries. We develop strange idiosyncrasies or moods to protect our psychic field from others. We look busy or disinterested so that nobody approaches us.

If this feels too isolating for us (too far into the desert) we go in the other direction and over compensate by becoming overly responsible for the people we love. This might look like empathy but it is really a recipe for unhappiness all round. One person falls into the sea and the other one jumps in after them. Now neither of them can get out, but at least they're united in their drowning experience. Suffering with someone isn't a form of compassion when you could do something useful, like inflate the life raft or go get help.

If we're going to break free of fusion and enjoy the wonders of flight by ourselves, we have to find the balance between empathy and dissociation. And if we're going to climb the mountain prior to take off we have to avoid the tendency to cling.

Climbing requires balance and faith. Each new handhold tempts us to stay where we are. This is what fusion looks like... clinging. In our ascent to higher consciousness, we cling like crazy to people (partners/children), products (food/alcohol), and ways of being (controlling/acquiescent). It's no wonder we can't give up a particular behavior or let go of a certain person, we're stuck like glue to them. Sometimes we give up the things we cling to briefly, only to replace them with a different version. We swop cigarettes for chocolate cake. We swop controlling other people to controlling the length of time on the treadmill. We swop one partner for another one. If we keep fusing to each handhold, we make very slow progress up the side of the mountain.

What's needed is industrial strength solvent. Luckily in the metaphysical dimension, there is solvent galore! This comes in the form of grace. If we un-prize our fingers and let go with courage instead of blind fear, grace will guide our hands to the perfect next position. Our climb can be enjoyable rather than distressing. Grace always makes the energy safe. It is the invisible safety harness, the transparent kite string. It stops us "freezing" and getting kidnapped by the bad guys.

The important thing is to breathe. Keep breathing. Funnily enough, this is also the advice they give you in childbirth.

On a wing and a prayer

DAY TWENTY SEVEN

I am in the middle of the countryside on the Mask making workshop. After so many disappointing workshops and seminars, I am pleased to report that this one is absolutely brilliant! I can now see the futility of using my mind to locate the lost bits of my psyche. The conscious mind doesn't want to see the unconscious – that's why it shoved it down there in the first place... duh! In blind faith, we send our mind out on missions. We imagine it is trawling through dark tunnels with a torch. In reality it is playing poker and listening to heavy metal music. Every now and then it pops up looking earnest and exhausted with nothing to report. No sight of anything. Like most military operations, our intelligence is flawed.

We need help from the good guys over in the right-brain!

> **Not self-help adage No. 27** Pop song (annoying in its original but re-crafted superbly by Joe Cocker) "I'll get by with a little help from my friends..."

It all starts with clay. I am in a room with five other women and a table piled high with art materials. The facilitator gives each of us a lump of clay to play with while we introduce ourselves and state our goals for the workshop. I brace myself for long boring tales of lives that bear no relation to mine and rehearse the "interested and concerned" expression I adopt when I'm not really listening.

Half an hour later I am surprised to find that I have so much in common with these women that, we could share the same DNA. While we are talking we knead and squish the clay like medieval peasants engaged in bread making. We have all spent most of our lives in modern careers, so this strange ritual somehow links us to a different time and place... one that existed before the take over bid by the left-brain. The theme that links all our stories is a vague dissatisfaction with life. We have "ticked all the boxes." We are successful, but there is very little joy in that success. We are on a treadmill that we can't get off. We are exhausted. In our attempts to distance ourselves from our parent's generation, we have created an empowered version of ourselves... but it is one that paradoxically has no power!

It feels good to immerse my hands in gooey grey sticky stuff. I push and pull at the clay while listening and talking. Suddenly the facilitator asks us to stop what we are doing and look at the strange assortment of shapes we have made. Mine started out as a long tube, which turned into a snake, then a snake eating its own tail, and finally a bread ring with fluted edges on top. As I look more closely it starts to resemble a garland of some kind – a scruffy crown for a fairy queen.

Now we have to draw the shape we have created - with our opposite hand! This is a huge stretch for six women who by and large define themselves as perfectionists. The left-brain is now screaming "It won't look right; that's rubbish; let me do it; use the other hand!" This is of course the strategy behind the exercise. Closing down the bully on the left and allowing the shy, quiet right-brain to venture gingerly onto the stage.

A vivid memory comes into my head. It is Christmas. My children are young and excited and desperate to help me decorate the tree. They reverently pick up baubles and silver flowers and tie them to the branches. I pronounce the effect "lovely" while inwardly feeling acute distress. For the rest of the evening I am distracted. I rattle through a bedtime story and as soon as they are asleep, go back to the tree and re-arrange every bauble into its correct place. I wire each tiny fairy light to the appropriate branch so that the beams perfectly illuminate the adjacent decoration. There is nothing random about my tree. I fall into bed exhausted. It is very late and no doubt I will be tired and slightly crotchety in the morning but the tree is perfection.

Looking back I want to cry. I missed the most precious part. Most of us do. Like industrious miners, toiling for long hours in the dark, we emerge triumphant with our basket of coal, only to discover that all along, we were surrounded by diamonds we couldn't see. I will never get back those evenings wasted on perfection. My children will never want that bedtime story again - the one in which I am totally present, the one where I can fully experience their excitement. I will never be able to look at a haphazard tree with wonky baubles and colors that just don't work and gaze in wonder at the early creative endeavors of my children.

It's time for a break. As I get to the end of a cup of coffee I notice I have eaten most of a packet of chocolate biscuits. The facilitator looks at me with compassion. She knows something is emerging and I am doing my level best to shove it back down again. Energy can stir things up and move them to the surface. But I have a strategy. Given enough sugar I can stop a volcano from erupting. My eyes meet those of the facilitator and I know the game is up. How much abuse can my body take before I realize that my left-brain is a rubbish strategist. What is it trying to create? Apart from the perfect diabetic of course.

Now it is time to make the actual masks. We divide into pairs; one lying on the floor while the other applies the plaster, carefully leaving the nostrils clear for breathing purposes. The plaster feels cold when it goes on but dries quickly, creating a strange sensation of separation from the outside world. The process is both messy kindergarten project and serious ancient ritual. When it is complete the mask comes away in one piece and there we are - six blank canvases awaiting an identity.

While the masks dry fully we go back to discussing the drawings. The facilitator wants us to decipher what they are communicating. This is a meaningless question when aimed at six left-brains. It is a long time since any of us were at kindergarten and we like things to fit within a structure that makes some sort of sense to us. Accessing the intelligence of the right-brain is like wandering around in a world without a map. We are uncomfortable when asked to "make things up" or "guess." What if they are wrong? Our desire to come up with the right answer or the best answer triggers memories of school. The glow and validation of getting things correct, and the humiliation and fear of getting them wrong.

Meanwhile the right-brain is bemused – after all everything over there is right! There are no wrong choices, there are just choices that don't have an agenda attached to them. I feel inspired to start writing again, just for the fun of it. This is what everyone needs - some help in getting past our personal agenda for order and logic so that we can reclaim our natural instinct to play in what the left-brain has defined as "chaos." Even the word "chaos" is frightening to most people, but that's just the rhetoric of the left. Compare "the fluidity of a world without straight lines." That's the same thing, but without the fear mongering.

What would it look like if we could stop controlling our world? If we stopped trying to be perfect. If we could just let go and allow ourselves to be carried. Where would the energy take us? Probably a far better place than the one we are in. We seem to have divided ourselves into two categories – those that fight and swim purposefully to their destinations and those that drift aimlessly. Letting go of control looks like aimless drifting, so obviously we don't want to do that. But once it is working properly, our internal GPS would reveal the truth - both control and drifting are equally ineffective strategies. They are two sides of the same coin.

To the mind, flowing with the energy and drifting without it, look exactly the same. We resist "flow" because we've programmed ourselves to be purposeful. The difference between "flow" and "drift" is the energy. Of course the mind can't detect energy. Energy can't be seen, heard or touched - it can only be felt. In order to feel energy we have to develop the intelligence of the heart.

This is a big problem for people who have closed off their heart in order to live in the lofty towers of the mind. They may have survived and been successful in the old world but they will be ill prepared for the one to come. A lot of smart businessmen died in the tsunami. A lot of seemingly dumb animals survived. They knew something that the executives didn't and that intelligence was not in their head. There are troubling times coming and if we are going to survive them, we need to start reading and interpreting the energy that surrounds us.

Our mind always think the solution lies in "more." If we have more military power, more brain power, more money, more resources then we'll become smart enough to figure out the answers to all our problems. But we don't need "more intelligence"; we need "better intelligence" - the intelligence of the heart. Our heart knows all about flow, and all about the power of friendship. If we can trust and follow, it will always lead us to a better place.

Better intelligence

DAY TWENTY EIGHT

Not self-help adage No. 28 but classic film line... 'Who was that masked man?'

The masks are dry and ready for decorating!

Looking at the table of art materials, my eye is drawn to a bowl of dried rose petals, faded to varying shades of dark red, dusty pink and pale brown. They remind me of the fairy Queen garland so I pick up a handful and start gluing them down one side of the mask. In between the flowers I paint dark green ivy leaves and pale green moss. This looks effective but rather tragic, like Ophelia floating in a watery grave, so I paint the other side of the mask with sweeps of bright orange and yellow paint. I glue gold sequins and attach bright feathers and a party streamer.

Standing back to admire the effect, I realize it is a perfect representation of the two parts of my mind – the party girl and the damsel. Looking around the room, it is amazing how different each mask is. There is a dark blue mask with gold feather, like an Indian princess; a soft lilac one with purple pipe cleaner eyebrows and sky blue hair ribbons; one covered in mirror sequined fabric like a Damien Hirst skull. They couldn't be more different if they tried. We all talk about what we see in each mask and the stories they reveal.

One of the women thinks my mask looks like Cassandra, the thwarted oracle of Greek mythology. As I am currently struggling with writer's block, this storyline has some resonance for me. Cassandra, though mortal, was a great favorite of the God Apollo who, during their romance, gave her the gift of prophecy. Sadly, their relationship hit a bad patch and lacking the necessary self-help book (that I have yet to write) things became very messy. Apparently the Gods can't take back the gifts they bestow, but they are pretty nifty with their curses. Apollo's parting shot to Cassandra was the curse that nobody would believe her.

Imagine having a talent you can't use! Imagine having something to say, but believing that nobody will want to hear it? How familiar does this sound? As I listen to this myth, I become acutely aware that there is another aspect of the story that resonates for me, one I have yet to write about! My boyfriend.

It's not like he's a big secret or anything. It's just that I sometimes wonder if he is a figment of my imagination. He is often away for long stretches of time. He's married to his work. He doesn't have a job, he has a vision and it's an all consuming 24/7 vision that allows very little time for a normal life. In fact he doesn't do "normal." A battalion of people sweat all his "small stuff". He flies around the world solving big problems for big people. In other words...

He is a God.

How interesting that the story of Cassandra could emerge from a lump of clay. Now that it is here I can start to trace its origins. My father is a charismatic man and (like many girls) I grew up attracted to alpha males onto whom I could project god like status. Of course when the men turn out to have feet of clay, things go horribly wrong and we are left with no partner and (like Cassandra) no means with which to express ourselves. We veer between admiration of the creativity in others (the god like creatures we project upon) and criticism of the creativity in ourselves (why will nobody notice me, listen to me - it must be because I'm not good enough.)

It isn't because we're not good enough, it's because we're under a spell.

What can we do to break the spell and get back our creative power? How do we change a pattern that is more appropriate to someone living in Athens circa 2000 B.C? If I'm comparing myself to a God, I'll never measure up. If I don't think anyone will believe or appreciate my book, it's no wonder I'm having a hard time writing it.

I am a frustrated Cassandra.

This block I'm having is not just about writing, it's about the thwarted dream of an Oracle. Why did I decide to write the book? If I look back at the beginning of this journal, it was because I wanted to help people by translating the metaphysical into the physical. I wanted to become a "Babel fish" for normal people; people who couldn't understand Ken Wilbur; people who found *Chicken Soup for the Soul* irritating; people who thought *The Secret* should have remained so. Not a Philosopher's stone for the enlightened, more a Rosetta stone for the rebellious.

I am quite excited by this new revelation. All I need to do now is figure a way to break the spell. A bonded (not fused!!) group of people is a great place to start. Talking. Deep listening. Revelation. Reflection. These are all great divination tools. Looking at the sad side of my mask I come up with an additional hidden belief – that the creative life could result in tragic death or madness. One of the other women gives voice to her belief that a creative life results in penury. The starving artist is a powerful archetype. Obviously, the more this pattern repeats itself through history, the more energy it attracts and the more power we need to break its spell.

It seems there are two parts to the equation of creative energy. First we need to allow the creativity to emerge. We have to trust that it wants to communicate with us and we have to develop tools to understand and interpret what it is saying. Next we have to be confident that we can deal with the "stuff" that this high voltage energy stirs up – all those pesky emotions and crazy beliefs. If our channels are clear, the creativity will be genuine.

Sue Congram, the workshop facilitator, deals with the first part of the equation by introducing exercises designed to mash up our senses. Remember the five senses that downloaded into the baby as a framework to enable it to interpret the new surroundings? We fused these senses with our perceptions until they became locked in and fixed. It takes a major event for us to go beyond this five sensory world. People who lose one of their senses develop heightened capacity in others but few of us can do this by our own efforts. Mashing up the senses can help relieve the deadlock.

We have to look at each part of the mask and try to discern a bodily sensation. We look at the color of the paint and wonder how it would move. We listen to a piece of music and imagine how it would like to be drawn. We imagine the shape of sounds by painting them in the air. We dance words. It sounds bonkers, and it is - to the left-brain. That's the point. Feeling a line; dancing a color; painting a piece of music. Suddenly the right-brain starts waking up from its long sleep.

And there isn't a Prince in sight!

As for the second part – dealing with the stuff the energy brings up – this requires practice and discipline. Energy doesn't require analyzing

- it just needs to be felt. Felt and released. I'm going to practice responding rather than reacting to the emotions in myself and other people. That means no displacement activity! (Could I really give up chocolate when I'm upset?) And no fixing other people when they're distressed! (Can I really sit with the feelings that come up, while my child searches yet again for her lost house keys?) Without a reaction, emotions run out of energy – they're just like small children really.

Marianne Williamson tells a funny story of a woman pushing a child having a tantrum in a supermarket trolley. "It's alright Sarah," she says while placing groceries in the basket. The child carries on screaming. "Don't worry Sarah, we're nearly there," she says while lining up in the queue to pay. The check out girl looks at her kindly and says "Sarah's very lucky to have you as a Mum" to which the bewildered woman replies "But I'm Sarah!"

We need to start being kind to ourselves. After all, the parts of us that are angry, confused and upset are probably about five years old. One thing's for sure... before we gain full access to our creativity, we need to nurture these under developed parts of our psyche. Why would the source of supreme creativity allow kindergarten children to play with electricity - they're not even allowed to run with scissors.

Time to send the kids to boot camp. Time to coax the damsel away from the lure of dark glamour and convince the party girl that more tequila isn't going to make anything better in the long run. Time to usher in the passion and skills of the Wise Woman.

We need to marshal our resources and get fighting fit if we're going to get enough power in the system to do what we need to do next...

Cast better spells than the ones we are under!

The three ages of Masks:
Disguise (the child)
Performance (the entertainer)
Ritual (the shaman)

DAY TWENTY NINE

Not self-help adage No. 29 Interlude Absorba the Greek...

I'm on my way home. Cassandra (my mask) is on the passenger seat integrating her dual personality. It's been an amazing couple of days and I feel back on track.

I decide to bone up on my Greek Mythology as soon as I get in. It is a fascinating subject.

***

First, there are a huge number of Greek Gods. For the ancient Greeks, this represented the many facets of the soul and the complex patterns of the universe. The Christians who only have two and a half Gods - God the father, God the son and God the Holy Ghost - all males, do not share this philosophy. Christians could be accused of a lack of imagination. There are numerous further examples of this scarcity of creativity, for example the songs of Cliff Richard and the inability to engage in metaphor.

At the very beginning of time there was Uranus (Heaven) and Gaia (Earth). They mated and produced the first race - the Titans - of which Cronos was the youngest. Uranus freaked out when he saw that his children were unattractive and made of flesh so he shut them up in the underworld. Gaia was FURIOUS. She fashioned a scythe out of flint and gave it to Cronos who hid in the shadows. When Uranus came to Gaia's bed, Cronos jumped out, castrated his father and threw his genitals into the sea. It was a slightly extreme response, but it served as another metaphor – sex goes underground.

Cronos then became the new King. He married Rhea. During his reign, the seasons; night and day; and all the cycles of nature were created. In fact this new era signaled the beginning of chronological time (which we get from Cronos.) However all was not well – Cronos was plagued by the prophecy that one of his sons would kill him. He couldn't accept this pattern repeat, so when Rhea gave birth to their first child, he swallowed the baby! Rhea became pregnant again and the same thing happened. After five years of this, Rhea was not best pleased so she hatched a cunning plan. Just before she was about to have her sixth child she ran away to Arcadia where she gave birth to Zeus, in a cave. Then she came home, wrapped a stone in a blanket and gave it to Cronos. He swallowed it - the stone and the story.

Years later, after Zeus had grown up, he returned home looking for vengeance. He appeared before Cronos disguised as a cupbearer and offered him a potion. Cronos swallowed (again!) and then proceeded to vomit. He threw up the five children and the stone. Miraculously all five children were UNHARMED. Thus began another new era - the reign of Zeus. Zeus made Mount Olympus. Cronos did not accede the throne willingly. War broke out between Cronos (with all the weird ugly Titans) and Zeus (with his mates the Olympians.) This was called the war of the Titans. Zeus won. His branding was just way better. Those rings on the white background... classic.

Zeus married Hera. There was harmony for a very short time. Zeus represented the masculine principle. Positive attributes - strength, focus and potency. Negative attributes - anger, self-righteousness and rigidity. Hera represented the feminine principle. Positive attributes - love, nurturing and creativity. Negative attributes eating too much chocolate cake and sulking.

Next came the FEMALE Gods. After Cronos castrated his father, he threw his genitals into the sea and the blood turned into lots more fairly insignificant Gods. However out of the sperm - or foam created from the turbulence, came the very significant Aphrodite. She emerged from the sea.

As a side bar... the Romans, who came after the Greeks, kept all the Greek Gods and just changed their names (more lack of imagination - probably too busy figuring out how to make those funny turtle shapes with their shields and auditioning for Gladiator). They called Aphrodite "Venus" and Botticelli immortalized her big entrance in a very expensive painting.

Aphrodite was so beautiful that Zeus was afraid she would cause trouble. To avoid all the gods fighting over her, he married her off to

Hephaestus. Hephaestus was a sort of dull "boy next door" God, a steady bloke, in fact a blacksmith. Aphrodite was so unhappy with this arrangement that she had a string of affairs, including one with Adonis that resulted in a love child - Eros (the Romans called him Cupid). Hephaestus was a good worker and made thunderbolts for Zeus, invincible armor for Achilles (worn so fetchingly by Brad Pritt in Troy) and a jeweled girdle for Aphrodite. This backfired as it made her even more beautiful.

The Romans called Hephaestus Vulcan, from volcano because he was the fire god... or possibly because he had pointy ears. Hephaestus also had a hand in creating the first human woman. Zeus had previously created humans but they were all males so Hephaestus fashioned a woman out of a bit of clay. She was called Pandora (which means "all gifts") and from her supernatural jar she released CHAOS (for chaos we can now read "choice and creativity") onto the human world. So women were blamed again for all the bad stuff that's going down.

Meanwhile Zeus (SUCH a player) was sleeping with everyone. He had an affair with Metis. Hera got angry and created a curse of her own - that Metis would bear a daughter, whose son would overthrow Zeus. When he found out about this spell Zeus promptly swallowed Metis before she could even give birth to the daughter. (This seems to be a recurring theme in Greek mythology.) When Hephaestus (who was Hera's son) found out, he was FURIOUS. He took an axe to Zeus's head and out popped Athena. Athena was quite an important Goddess, as she was the only one born from a male form. She was a brilliant warrior and strategist, presumably because she had no pesky emotions getting in the way of a good plan.

I have now been reading for some time but can't stop. Greek mythology is the perfect antidote to my insomnia. I make some hot chocolate, add a slug of whiskey and return to bed. Early fireworks are going off outside. It feels quite cozy to be inside wrapped in a duvet with a good book. Cassandra is perched on the bedside table beside me. I carry on...

Three of the most symbolic figures in Greek mythology were all sons of Cronos.

Zeus - God of the Sky

Poseidon - God of the Sea

Hades - God of the Underworld.

This could be a metaphor for the conscious, subconscious and unconscious mind. The territories of sky, sea and underworld were mapped out by The Three Fates. (The Romans called them The Three Graces). They were the spinner, the measurer and the cutter. Even the gods were subject to them. These fates designed each person's contract then wove it with certain gifts, limitations and challenges to overcome.

This seems to me, an alternative trinity to the Father, Son and Holy Ghost. The female trinity cuts the templates (our archetypes), spins some lovely gifts (our natural talents) and creates some challenges for good measure.

Of course, every now and then both gods and humans think they know better. This is always BAD NEWS as the Three Fates are big on HUBRIS. (It's their little way of saying "I don't think so.") The Three Fates are feminine - another reason to write girls out of history or burn them at the stake when they get a bit uppity. They came back for a cameo appearance in "The Minority Report."

Back to Cronos (father of Zeus, Hades and Poseidon.) After he vomited up Posei and the family stone, Cronos realized he'd been tricked, and rushed off, mad as hell looking to kill Zeus. Along the way he met a mortal called Philyra who he tried to mate with. She didn't want anything to do with him. *(Aren't you that weird baby eating guy?)* She ran away, while pleading with the other Gods to change her shape. They obliged by turning her into a HORSE. Cronos trumped this by changing himself into a horse - only one that gallops faster, so he nailed her anyway. Months later she gave birth to Chiron who was a Centaur - not only was he half man half horse; he was also half mortal half god. (First evidence of identity crisis and the beginning of the world of duality). Philyra was horrified and didn't want to raise the child beasty thing so she begged the Gods to transform her again. They change her into a TREE... she was possibly hoping for something a little more animated but what can you do.

Zeus of course went on to defeat Cronos in the war of the Titans, and Cronos was relegated to the underworld. Chiron was thus left orphaned and alone, until he met two new friends, both sons of Zeus: Apollo who mentored him in the Mysteries - the arts of healing, music, prophecy and divination; and Heracles (the Romans called him

Hercules) who had recently returned from slaying the nine headed hydra. During some manly joshing about, Chiron was accidentally wounded with the tip of one of Heracles arrows (which contained the deadly poisonous blood of the hydra.) Though in pain (he was half mortal) he could not die (because he was half immortal.)

Chiron went off searching for a cure. Despite being tutored by Apollo in the healing arts, he could not heal himself; however on his journey he healed many others. He was in effect therefore the first "wounded healer". How many of us today are better at helping others than we are able to help ourselves? Curiously enough, in 1977 a new planet was discovered orbiting between Saturn and Uranus. Scientists named it Chiron. Subsequent to this we entered the "therapy era," a time when many people lay on couches seemingly unable to heal their wounds. So, we should be careful how we name things. Carl Jung would call this synchronicity.

Meanwhile Prometheus (one of the Titan Gods) started to take pity on the humans. At that time the humans lived in caves and ate raw meat. Gods came down and had sex with their women. He decided to bring them the gift of FIRE, which metaphorically would give them illumination and also allow them to barbecue their meat. Prometheus therefore stole the sacred fire from the Gods and brought it to the humans. Zeus was FURIOUS. As punishment Prometheus was chained to a rock on a mountain where an eagle pecked out his liver. Because he was immortal, at the end of the day a new liver formed and the following day he would have to endure the whole process all over again. This punishment went on for 30 years... !

Chiron (half god half human) who by now was bored with his particular brand of pain, offered to take Prometheus's place on the rock. Zeus was so moved by this selfless act of sacrifice that he immortalized Chiron and made him into a fully-fledged God. Yay!... because clearly we need more of them!

And what's Poseidon been up to during this time? He was also befriending the humans, in particular a man called Minos. With Poseidon's help, Minos became King of Crete. In return Poseidon wanted Minos to sacrifice a beautiful white bull in his honor. Minos was now on a bit of an ego trip. He didn't want to sacrifice the lovely bull so he offered up a rubbish animal instead, thinking he could get away with it.

Poseidon was FURIOUS and asked for Aphrodite's help in humiliating him. She cast a spell on Minos's wife, which caused her to form a consuming passion for the white bull! The wife bribed Daedalus the carpenter to build a wooden cow. (You really couldn't make the next bit up) and she climbed inside the wooden cow so that the white bull could enter her. Months later she gave birth to the MINOTAUR! (A hideous creature with a man's body and a bull's head who ate human flesh.) Minos was suitably shamed... well who would want to turn up at the school gate and own up to this offspring, not to mention the trauma of packing the lunchtime Tupperware. He ordered Daedalus to build a labyrinth to contain the creature.

We therefore have Daedalus to thank for all the those circular walkways, which are such a feature of new age seminar centers. No wonder the delegates are all over the place... these things were designed to hide some very bad shit, not to locate your inner shinola.

Eventually of course the Hero Theseus, son of Poseidon, falls in love with Ariadne, daughter of Minos and he goes in and slays the Minotaur. Poseidon was FURIOUS and created an earthquake burying King Minos. Theseus then became King of Crete and married Ariadne.

Cue: 'There's a place for us'.

Fade to black.

I turn off bedside lamp. if I don't sleep now I never will. Even Cassandra is nodding off, and she's related to these people.

Bad boys, bad boys, what ya gonna do...

DAY THIRTY

Self-help adage No. 30 **Intimacy... into me see**

I slept all through the night! Something has shifted in my psyche. Psyche of course is another Greek word, which didn't fare well when it married our left-brain and became psych-ology. It seems I have made peace with the random world of the unconscious by giving it airtime. Greek mythology is now flying around with the kites in the park, showing off its long tail.

I turn on the computer and check the emails. Chloe is planning a weekend road trip with her flat mates. Simon seems to have drifted into interstellar space and she is no longer caught in the magnetics of his orbit. Good. While she is away, she is going to plot her TV drama. Perhaps she will fall in love all over again. I send her greetings from Hermes who is the God of travelers, funny silk scarves and very expensive luggage.

There are three emails from my fabulous boyfriend, aka Apollo, all from different locations – a car, an airport lounge and the tarmac of some runway where the stewardess nymphs all turn a blind eye to the fact that his blackberry is still on.

It's quiet in the house, but not uncomfortably so. It's a time for reflection. I had thought that the journey to reclaim my lost creativity was one of discovery but I'm increasingly aware that it's one of balance. Creativity is always turned on, but we can't hold center long enough to allow it to find us, plus we now know that the center has different levels – conscious, subconscious and unconscious.

On the conscious level there's the balancing of neediness and control, played out by the damsel and the knight. On the subconscious level there's the balancing of fear and trust, played out by the orphan child and the magical child. But delving even further into the unconscious, where is my sense of balance between Cassandra and Apollo? The further we dive into the unconscious realm, the closer we get to the fulcrum – the balance between the soul and the ego. The soul loves unity and equality. The ego loves competition and comparison.

Equality with Apollo? I look at my surroundings – amongst the coffee mugs and plates of toast crumbs, there are endless "to do" lists, emails to answer, things that need fixing and notes on the book I have still to write. Imagining I am my boyfriend's equal is a stretch to say the least. He doesn't struggle with writer's block, he just passes his hands over the keyboard and hundreds of perfect words appear on the screen. He has no battles with technology, it does his bidding. His computer doesn't crash, his phone always has a signal and he knows what buttons to press on the television remote. It's enough to make you want to give up, but we've dealt with the tantrum child so that's no longer an option.

Competition and comparison are roadside bombs on the road to creativity. We write something we're happy with, then we read something that makes us weep with envy. I don't have shoe envy or even status envy, I have sentence envy. How do we feel equal with our Gods? Bruce Springsteen is a cool, laid back guy. He works hard at remaining so. I don't know how he does this - perhaps he has created an airport style security desk that requires him to check in his ego before he leaves the house. The "God" thing certainly doesn't come from him. He carries no thunderbolts in the back pocket of his Levis. So how come it's impossible to meet him and not be struck dumb. Why are we scared to make eye contact? Do we think we'll be blasted like Paul off his donkey? What happens to us?

People who live in the creative energy of "now" are immensely attractive. They've got something we desperately want if only we could let go of our attachments. Apollo has no problem letting go, but then being a God, he isn't attached to anything.

In similar fashion, Buddhists have made an entire spiritual practice out of non-attachment. They don't need one intimate soul mate; they are in harmony with all things. Their primary relationship is with the God in everybody. This seems a lonely existence to me. I want to be in harmony with everything, but I'd like to be able to share that harmony with another person. I know form is an illusion but it's a lovely illusion and one that I don't want to give up just yet.

So if we create our own reality, how come I've created a relationship with a safe amount of distance – both horizontal (separation by air miles) and vertical (separation by height of pedestal!)? It must be that damn ego again. As always, the ego has a slightly different take on the philosophy of non-attachment. It produces its own counterfeit version - non-commitment. It's a strategy that has become very popular in the western world.

Whilst our left-brain is happy to make a commitment to a job, it struggles with making a commitment to another person. Jobs are easy to control but people are full of emotions, which are difficult to control, to say the least. Now that western women have experienced the joys of job commitment, we've become a little unstuck in the relationship department. If we all choose fulfillment through a career, what happens to the children? They're usually not quite so keen on the idea of non-attachment.

So what are we so afraid of?

The answer is of course "Intimacy." Intimacy is our ability to be in relationship with high voltage energy. This is the kind of energy that comes through two people in a truly equal partnership. Their unity acts as both earthing rod and container for the upgraded energy. It's both our dream come true and our worst nightmare.

The ego (CEO of "Worst Nightmare Scenario") advises against unity. It recommends unequal relationships, in which we are either "in control" of the other, or the other is "in control" of us. ("They'll do for now" vs. "we are not worthy") This results in lots of low voltage power struggles, which dilute the energy and cause endless outages. This isn't great, but we are comfortable with low voltage energy – it doesn't scare the pants off us.

If we are ready to form an equal relationship, the ego creates all sorts of barriers in order to maintain a safe distance. These can be literal - long-distance relationships; or metaphoric - tricky situations involving ex partners. One of the features of modern relationships is the difficulty of defining our status – Single? Married? Many people are calling for a new category called "It's complicated."

The ego, being the principle of separation, always recommends distance. It tells us that if we get very close to another person, our molecules will merge with theirs and we'll get sucked into a black hole. We'll cease to exist as a "separate self." (Our ego reads a lot of science fiction). Our spirit is trying to tell us that if we get into a relationship with another and re-channel all the emotional energy that comes up, we could be on the super highway to blissful intimacy in no time at all. We wouldn't need to climb to the top of hills to appreciate the view, we could do vertical take off from the ground.

We just need to lose our fear of high voltage energy.

This energy takes two forms – creativity and love. When we are able to vessel the energy of pure creativity or pure love, we are "carried away" by the experience. We are certainly no longer in control. With this form of creativity we could do more than write a book or paint a picture, we could solve all those complex world problems we have inadvertently created with our left-brains. With this form of love we could create more than a marriage of opposites – we could achieve the divine union that our souls are yearning for.

Do we need any more persuading?!

If we are going to vessel this energy, we have to do our part in getting our vehicle fit for purpose:-

1. We need to become comfortable with nakedness. Physical intimacy requires nakedness. Sex is much better when we overcome our shyness and fully express our sexual energy. Creativity and Love require its metaphysical counterpart – transparency. In other words, we have to get comfortable about showing up and revealing our inner essence. Our natural inclination is to hide our creative spirit, while praying for divine inspiration. This is a little like trying to have sex through many layers of clothing and is a very ineffective way to become pregnant with a good idea.

2. We need to become comfortable with energy. Our natural inclination is to "play tennis" with the energy. If someone does something for us, we immediately want to do something in return for them. If someone says something, we immediately start thinking of our response. We are hopeless at receiving and holding energy. As far as sex is concerned, magazines are full of advice

about technique and how to "do" great sex – not how to receive great sex. Being tied up (literally) is the only way we allow this to happen – then it appears to be happening against our will. We need the subterfuge of bondage to bypass our own mind!

How can we help ourselves to receive better?

By becoming honest about the private agendas of our ego. Creativity and love require honesty. Owning up to the fact that we are jealous, insecure and self interested is powerful. Then we can start to change. Becoming honest and clearing up our inner mess makes getting naked much easier, as we have nothing hideous to hide, nothing to feel guilty or ashamed about.

By allowing ourselves to feel vunerable. This requires practice. Holding onto the energy of feeling vulnerable and exposed, while resisting the urge to deflect the energy is very empowering. It's yet another paradox of the energetic realm.

If we can hold the energy (by not reacting to another's behavior, not responding immediately to dialogue) something happens. The easiest way to describe this is that the energy moves from our mind into our heart. Everything feels different. The energy becomes richer and the experience of the present moment becomes more meaningful. The greater meaning we are searching for in the outside world is in fact within us. We have the potential to forge a different relationship with whatever is going on, thus creating more meaning in everything. We are surrounded by new information. Things we would have dismissed or simply not been aware of, become highly relevant. Our intelligence increases.

Though our mind is fixed, our heart is capable of expansion, so can vessel the greater intelligence on offer. The intelligence of the mind comes from knowledge and data, which emanates from the past. The world is changing so fast that the past is increasingly irrelevant. The intelligence of the heart is totally up to date and inseparable from the present moment, so is totally appropriate to what is emerging.

Any action we subsequently take is far more wise and inclusive.

The Internet is a wonderful tool that enables us to connect up and become a global species, but like everything it is only as good as its users. It allows us to share our ideas and build meaningful tribes i.e. those based on common interest rather than accidents of birth. But unless we grow up and use it wisely, it can become a means to hide. We are able to create in the privacy of our home and then launch our creations onto the web when they're ready. The most powerful aspect of street art, street theatre, and stand up comedy is the raw experience of working with "live" energy. This allows constant immediate feedback in the present moment – a raised eyebrow, a pregnant pause, a bored sigh. It enables us to morph and change along with it, co-creating with the energy in a constant series of "now" moments.

This is life in its truest sense of the word – a life in which we feel alive. It's not a state of mind.

It's intimacy.

I look at Cassandra, who is now propped up on my desk. Like many frustrated women she eventually lost her mind – and not in a good way! She is willing me to become smart enough to break the spell she has been under for 2000 years. I've got a feeling that when she wakes up she'll bring all the power necessary to deal with whatever comes next.

But first I need to re-negotiate terms with Apollo.

The magnetism of Apollo

DAY THIRTY ONE

It is 5am. A beam of light pulses from my mobile phone. I can't go back to sleep. My thoughts are already as unruly as a bunch of pirates, revealed by the mini lighthouse on the bedside table. I could be writing instead of lying here in the dark. The phone pings with another text message from Apollo. He is helping global leaders make better decisions. I am trying to figure out whether to make coffee or doze for another hour.

I remember yesterday's pledge to stop making comparisons and stumble into the kitchen to make the coffee.

The worst thing about the departure of my children and, more recently the departure of Chloe, is that I am acutely aware of how hopeless I am at actually putting into practice the things that I preach. It's so much easier to coach others. I was really positive when I went to bed. How can a three-line text message take all my power away?

I need to pull myself together. Unity consciousness with another is a rubbish aspiration if the fragments of your own consciousness are all over the place. Perhaps I need to look at the ground zero of my chakra system. In energetic terms, this is the root chakra.

> ***Self-help adage No. 31*** **Not the Odyssey of ancient Greece (!) more the Odissey of ancient discotheques. 'Going back to my roots… yeah'.**

If we want to vessel high voltage energy, we need to be properly "earthed" otherwise (as we have seen) we will attach ourselves to the earthing rods of other people. We can't master the skills of balance if we don't have a strong platform to balance on. Once we achieve balance, we can hold steady while the inspiration comes in through the top of our head and makes its way to the earth beneath our feet.

Images of inspiration were once depicted purely in terms of the spiritual - most early art has a religious theme. The inspiration usually came in the form of prophecy – a kind of "to do" list that was hand delivered by angels. The recipients of the inspiration had a halo around their crown chakra – which served as an early 'high voltage' symbol.

During the past few hundred years of left-brain dominance we extended the definition of inspiration to include "visitations" to the genius mind. To qualify for this inspiration, one required focus and discipline, rather than spiritual devotion. Inspiration came to academics, engineers, musicians and other super clever people.

Now our beliefs have changed again. We all want access to daily inspiration and we are not convinced this comes about purely from dedication – either to prayer or career. The price of entry is not something we have to get; it's something we have to lose - our fear of accountability for the inspiration. Because once we receive a download of inspiration, we usually have to do something with it!

Turning inspiration into form is a kind of alchemy. Leonardo da Vinci had thousands of ideas, very few of which made it into any kind of form. Perhaps he just loved hanging out in the energy of inspiration and had no attachment to seeing his ideas take shape in the physical world. We, on the other hand, derive most of our enjoyment from the transformation process of thought into form. The inability to execute our ideas creates a logjam in our body, which can lead to depression. Our creativity dries up and leaves us feeling powerless. If we want more creativity we have to become skilled at turning thought into form.

I can't go back to sleep so I put on some clothes, and head off for an early morning walk in the park.

There are two more dials on *The Sextant* that need addressing. We all want to "be somebody" and we all want to "do something significant." We jump at the "doing" part but we lack the energy to pull it off because we need to get comfortable with the "being" part first.

The blueprint of our "being" is located in the root chakra. When we're born we have everything in place to guarantee success with our chosen destiny. Obviously this is in seed form as we are quite small. In an ideal world, as we grow, so would our talents, allowing us to "be creative" in our chosen field. However we seem to be living in some weird reverse pantomime world where we trade our talents. We give away our magic beans in exchange for a cow – usually a cash cow! Our left-brain is just *too* logical - cows provide more food than beans... and we don't believe in magic.

Enter Jack! We need to become a principled boy if we are going to reverse this tale. Get back the seeds of our original talents. Sew them, nurture them, and climb the beanstalk to the creative realm.

I could do with some more coffee but I'm now stuck in the park with my rambling mind. Perhaps a walking meditation would help. Who am I kidding? Walking with no thoughts was certainly not a talent bestowed on me at birth by the gift fairy.

How to return to being? To get at the root chakra, our mind wants to trawl through our childhood, but this is a trap. The mind is useless at being. We need to listen to the body. I look at the text from Apollo and see how it makes me feel – exasperated and inadequate. There's tension in my throat and a leaden feeling in my solar plexus. Keeping well away from my mind I make a new choice – to run the energy out of my body. Literally.

I take off my coat, wrap it around my bag and leave it under a huge oak tree. Then I start running. My body feels stiff and the cold air hurts my lungs, but I keep going. Soon I develop a rhythm. Oxygen floods into my body. My muscles warm up but there's resistance in my lungs. I keep going. The lungs stop fighting as they realize I am serious – or perhaps my mind has been knocked out by the surfeit of oxygen and can no longer send messages. Either way I realize something amazing.

I have stopped thinking.

Time passes. I have no idea how long I've been running but eventually I make my way back to the oak tree and sitting on my coat, lean back against the bark. Endorphins are now running through my system and I smile involuntarily. My chest rises and falls but I am not breathing. I am being breathed. My mind has stopped altogether.

I'm so happy I could die! Taking out my phone I look at the text from Apollo. Nothing. No animation in my body. The part of my psyche that I am now inhabiting has no problem whatsoever. It is happy just being. It's also happy with however everything else in life is choosing to be in this moment. The dog walker with the sharp voice, the small spiders scurrying around the tree roots. The wind, which can't make up its mind which way to blow... and Apollo.

Learning "how to be" is all about developing soul esteem. The esteemed soul doesn't need to do things in order to feel better. It doesn't need to achieve goals in order to gain approval. It does things because it is inspired to do them, because it is curious, because it wants to have a delicious experience of living.

Inspiration and action can become a seamless duo if there is no agenda of expectation (i.e. expecting a result in which we look good and bask in the approval of others.) Goals and expectations set us up for a life of disappointment, whereby we miss the main event, because we're always looking some place else. We are literally living in our heads. If we pay attention to the present, we can be helped in all kinds of ways – from the intuition in our gut and the intelligence in our heart.

Unless we have aspirations to be a mad professor or a hysterical Cassandra, we need to learn to become good conductors of energy. We don't want to stay up in the clouds where the air is thin and the companions are few. We can become lightning rods, clear channels through which the energy can move from inspiration, above our head to manifestation beneath our feet.

There are a lot of trees in Richmond Park. Some of them fell in the last hurricane. They form strange sculptures on which children play - branches on one side, and spaghetti of roots on the other. The soil is hard. The roots grow horizontally, so cannot hold in a strong wind. We are living in stormy times. We need to dig deep, go back to our roots and replant them firmly in the ground.

Then we can truly become inspired.

Deep roots and flexibility trump strength

DAY THIRTY TWO

Self-help adage No. 32 "We" are one.

I'm feeling much better this morning. Had long lovely phone conversation with Apollo last night. Was able to hear his litany of achievements with no trace of remorse!

I engage in my morning ritual of coffee and mail opening - mostly junk and bills including one from Visa that extends to two pages. Barclaycard is trying to rival my word count! I turn on the computer - the usual flyers for books and workshops offering the secrets of the universe, the healing of illness, the personal counsel of archangels and the skinny on quantum physics in three days for under two hundred dollars with a money back guarantee.

My bin is full of paper. My inbox is full of sappy aphorisms that I need to forward to at least ten people in the next five minutes or risk three lifetimes of bad karma. It's hard not to pull up the last romantic missive from Apollo and lapse into the fantasy realm. *Stay present. Be here now.* I feel the need for cake. Cassandra gazes impassively from the work surface. No cake for breakfast. If my current carbohydrate addiction carries on at this pace, "Mama Cass" might be a more appropriate moniker.

A quick scan of the world news reveals nothing positive. Endless stories of celebrities to feed our insatiable appetite for how the other half lives and infinite examples of collective stupidity that demonstrate the foolishness we ordinary mortals have to put up with. There is a story about the growth in crime. Various people are interviewed including legislators and leaders of charitable organizations. Individually they all sound so intelligent, yet the outcome of their collaborative endeavors is staggeringly inept. I suppose it's just like a romantic relationship - brilliant while there's separation and dating, hopeless when there's collaboration and marriage. It's all those unconscious agendas again - the prison break molecules that rush to the surface.

We need creativity!

Then or course there's the difficulty of making decisions in any collaborative endeavor. That's always a recipe for disaster.

I remember "creative" meetings in advertising. They would usually start with an idea. Various people in the meeting would want to put their stamp on the idea to justify their involvement, other people would criticize the idea to show their superior knowledge, and others would query it to establish the indispensible nature of their department or adapt it because it was over budget. Yet more people would over ride this and double the budget because it is was now late. The final result? A watered down, overpriced mess that bore no relation to the original idea. Because everyone wanted to have an opinion.

The need to have an opinion stems from the desire to have verification that we exist, or more accurately (given our left-brain dominance) endorsement that we exist more vividly than others.

The media are the worst culprits of this "need to have an opinion" thing. They have to keep up a running commentary. When there's nothing to say, they find a way of saying nothing. This usually involves a variety of the following - criticizing, justifying, speculating and elaborating.

Bad stuff happens, but it happens once. When we make it into opinion and blast it 24/7 through hundreds of media channels, it happens countless times over and over again in our minds. That's a lot of negative energy floating around the collective. We are frightened about what might happen and we're furious about the inability of laws and regulations to protect us from bad stuff, whether this is street crime or the more sophisticated type of mugging from Wall Street Bankers.

This is a total drain on our creative energy.

Let's go back to the transparency of intimacy. Imagine if collectively we could become skilled at reading energy. The energy can't lie and it can't hide. It is the arbiter of truth. Long ago this used to be called conscience. In our quest for consciousness we forgot all about conscience. Now it needs an upgrade. Conscience, in the past, was linked to fear. What will *they* think? What will *God* think?

God doesn't think (duh!) and God isn't interested in our goodness if it comes from fear or a desire to look good. The source of supreme creativity doesn't pay a whole lot of attention to lip service, as the frequency of this vibration is too low – it doesn't show up on the cosmic radar. Therefore no high voltage creativity and inspiration is available. Shame really as...

We need creativity!

And as for the bad stuff that might happen - of course things go wrong in our world but whipping people up into a frenzy of fear is just not helpful now that we know the mechanics of how energy works. Worrying is using our imagination to create something we don't want. We need to hone our imagination and use it for something much more inspired. We have this amazing opportunity to create, if only we could stop ourselves being "taken over by the fear." And, our other dysfunctional behavior – attempting to legislate our way to safety - is equally bonkers.

A friend of mine is a brilliant, successful businessman. He also happened to grow up in a violent family, had a difficult relationship with authority figures and spent time in a correctional facility. There is not a person on the planet more suited to speak to young offenders about their predicament and the various creative ways they could emerge from the corners they have boxed themselves into. He offered his mentoring services free of charge. He was turned down. He didn't have the right degree qualification and needed to go through a lengthy vetting procedure. For what? In case he corrupted criminal minds with his optimism? In case he harmed them? These people were sharing cells with convicted rapists.

When will legislators figure out the futility of most laws? The vulnerable people in society are babies and children. Yet anyone can have a baby. Crack addicts, pedophiles and people with a history of violent behavior frequently do. It's not politically correct to make a law preventing this happening, so we compensate by protecting damaged teenagers from social entrepreneurs and schoolchildren from Grandmothers (who are unable to help them read without a qualification).

Where is common sense? Apparently it's not so common. When will we learn to trust our intuition? What would conscience look like for the 21st century? Not the false morality of the mind, more the conscientiousness of the heart. We need a new banner to rally around and a new marketing tool to promote it.

And like a fairy godmother, the source of supreme creativity tapped Tim Berners-Lee on the head with her magic wand and pronounced, "You shall create the world wide web!"

Luckily Sir Tim was "open for business" on that day. Imagine if his creative channels were filled with the negative gunk of mind paralyzing bad news. The course of human evolution could have had a severe setback.

The computer screen linked to the Internet is like a 3D version of our energy system. The only difference is that when we press "send" on a computer keyboard, we believe that our thoughts appear on the other side of the world. We should trust the power of our thoughts to do the same without the hardware interface.

Inspiration has provided the Internet. We need to do our bit now by using it to connect with others to collaborate in more meaningful ways. As Apollo is fond of saying "We need to create WE." Whenever we talk about the lack of common sense and the broken systems, we always put "we" at the beginning of the sentence.

Who is this "we"? Where are we? How many of us are there? We may not be represented by governments or institutions or the media, yet we're a powerful force. Governments depend on us – they are nothing without our vote. Corporations depend on us – they are nothing without our purchasing power. And as for the media, in the wake of blogging and you tube, you could say...

WE are the media.

There are no better words

DAY THIRTY THREE

Global dilemma No. 33 (perfectly summed up by Diana Ross) "We're in the middle of a chain reaction"

My 40 day intention is working! I am finding it much easier to write. By the time I get to the last few days there will be steam rising from my fingers as they fly across the keyboard. This image summons a wistful reverie of Apollo, who is currently in darkest Africa doing something important. Africa attracts visionaries. Or rather very complex problems attract visionaries and Africa has more than their fair share of them - Aids, poverty, injustice, mad dictators, corruption, and crime.

In reality, as in all things holistic, we have the third world we deserve. If we have a dual mindset, not a "we are all one" mindset, we create winners and losers both in our personal relationships and in the world at large. The idea of competition starts very early on for us so is at the deepest level of our mind. The thought "If I don't get my needs met, I won't survive" is at the root of all problems – both personal and global.

From an evolutionary point of view we have always known that we play "win lose." At the physical level, it was survival of the fittest - this was hand-to-hand combat stuff and the losers were usually left on the battlefield. We then went on to the mental level, where it was survival of the smartest – our empire building days left the losers toiling away in sweatshops and living in slums. However now that we are entering the energetic level, we are on the verge of something new – survival of the "creatives."

In a world where physical labor comes cheap and mental work can be replaced by technology, creativity is King. This goes for any line of work. Practical skills can be learnt, but creativity is an attitude, a way of being. It requires a willingness to be open to inspiration, to engage and take risks. Our past measure of job fitness was an enthusiasm for "doing" – working late, heroic numbers of emails and the endurance test of modern travel. But that just doesn't cut it anymore. The race for creative supremacy is on.

In ancient times people dealt with their survival fears by huddling together and forming tribes. In the 1960s, hippies resurrected the idea and formed communes. Both models relied on a certain level of consciousness i.e. primitive or stoned. Surviving happily in a tribe used to require the abdication of personal power and "buy in" to collective beliefs. With the advent of the Internet, the concept of a tribe has taken on new meaning, allowing us to bypass geographic and cultural barriers.

The source of supreme creativity likes the harmony of tribes, but not at the cost of inspiration. Now that we have huge global problems we need huge global creativity. The Internet is also helping to facilitate this by disengaging creativity from the "middle man" of agent, publisher or patron. However the "win/lose" dynamic of fear and scarcity is still rife. We are overwhelmed by social media as the urge to "share" our knowledge, art or trivia makes us compete even more.

How do we turn creativity from highly competitive to global phenomenon?

Our last collective surge in creativity happened between the 14th and 17th centuries, during the Renaissance. The invention of money and the banking system played a big part in freeing up creativity. Prior to this we traded – food, textiles, spices, gold, labor. A lot of energy was expended in the day-to-day business of staying alive. If we had nothing to trade with, we didn't survive.

Money changed the game. Money has no intrinsic value - it's a promissory note that acts as a medium of exchange. As such, it's an energy that "allows" things to be created (a bit like the intangible quality of self-esteem allows things to be created.) During the Renaissance, artists, scientists, entrepreneurs sponsored architects and astronomers and the world benefited from amazing works of art and feats of engineering.

We know money doesn't actually exist. We understand that we can't ask for our money or the global financial system would collapse overnight. Yet our belief in the power of money is so strong that we are willing to operate under its spell. We think it is the only way we will be able to continue evolving, even though we are aware that most countries are bankrupt and that it's now mathematically impossible to pay off the US national debt!

Money doesn't work anymore. Money, like electricity, is neutral. Its expression in the physical world can have good and bad consequences. Our consciousness level is currently not adequate to manage the energy because we are still playing win/lose. The fear and scarcity created by win/lose acts as a circuit breaker for the energy. This turns the energy to matter, as stealing and hoarding become commonplace. The waves become particles. We need to replace money with a different mechanism or we need to change our perception to re-engage at the wave level.

How do we turn creativity from a solo pursuit to a collaborative one?

There is a biblical quote "Where two or more are gathered together, in my name, I am there". It plays out as follows. Two boys playing guitars not particularly well in separate locations meet up, usually in somebody's garage. The source of supreme creativity rocks up as promised. Lennon and McCartney go on to produce a bazillion brilliant songs. There is disharmony of course, as they find it difficult to get along with each other (no strategy for the crazy molecules.) Eventually the need for harmony wins over the joy of inspiration, and they go their separate ways to pursue solo careers. John Lennon becomes a recluse and Paul McCartney writes the frog chorus. Meanwhile their back catalogue joins the ranks of the eternal (obviously as something eternal was involved in the creation process).

If we want to live a creative life we have to figure out a better way of dealing with the win/lose conflict and get to inspired collaboration. Globally of course the win/lose dynamic has far worse consequences than the proliferation of bad pop songs.

So back to Africa, where our evolutionary history began and where it's all coming full circle. We have tried throwing money at Africa. This hasn't been an effective strategy because, as we now know, money itself has no value, it's the intention (i.e. the thoughts behind the strategy) that create the results. Some of our intentions have been slightly suspect. We're scared that if they start winning, it'll be our turn to lose. We want the problem to go away, so that we don't have to see it on the nighttime news. We need to feel better about ourselves. We dissociate.

Hmmm... but now we want to be creative. Dissociation and creativity are a contradiction in terms of energy. If we want to be creative, we have to become present and this means we have to be ok with what is. We have to "be" with what is, up close, without going into reaction. It doesn't matter if our reaction is good (raise money, do something) or bad (dissociate, do nothing.) When our reaction is driven by fear or discomfort, the outcome is ineffective.

If we can be with what is, and feel the feelings in our body, something happens. The feelings give way to the deeper feelings. If we stick with this energy, without going into resistance, it eventually disperses and a new, inspired thought arises. Now we can act. If we clear our inner space, our actions will be co-creative, rather than ego enhancing schemes of grandiosity or sacrifice. We can respond to situations instead of reacting to them.

We think we're so smart that we have all the answers but Africa has much to teach us. Our philosophies are impregnated with win/lose. "Survival of the fittest." "Be the best." Compare this with their original philosophy of "Ubuntu" in other words "We become in the presence of others." or "I am because we are."

Apollo is doing his level best to deal with the outcome of hundreds of years of win/lose choices. He is on a crusade. I am being supportive overseas girlfriend. It's quite a medieval image. Perhaps I could weave him a sextant to complete the picture - forget about writing the book. I'm momentarily taken with a Lady of Shallot type vision. Having worked in advertising, I know how to spin. Imagine what I could create with some magic thread. But these days are over. We're in the middle of a chain reaction. With a world in crisis, the present moment has no room for disco divas or mad dictators and certainly no room for damsels.

Adewale Ajadi – Visionary Leader

DAY THIRTY FOUR

Self-help adage No. 34 Home is where the heart is…
(or was a long long time ago)

Thomas Wolfe once said, "You can never go home again." Of course you can physically go (I arrived here this morning) but Tom was referring to something else. Places that we revisit are never the same - not because they have changed, but because we have.

The acid test of whether we've pulled up and released enough of the stuck energy in our body is to spend time with our family of origin. It's easy to show emotional maturity in the office but it's another matter to maintain your equilibrium in your childhood home. Statistical analysis for the Christmas holiday season reveals peak levels of divorce, addiction, depression and suicide. Our original families can be seen as a nightmare to be avoided, or a high level spiritual challenge with equally high-level rewards. They are an opportunity to see what's tangled up at the deepest levels… in our roots.

It's natural for us to separate from our parents and evolve into "who we are" – but if there is no graceful way to accomplish this we often resort to rebellion. We reject our parent's values and ideas and embrace our own. But then we stamp a brand on both identities and they become fixed and incompatible. A visit home becomes a stand off between a Mac and a PC user. We both become preoccupied with our branded version of reality rather than reality, and we are no longer able to articulate the layers of subtlety between the two. If our version of God is "creative spirit in all of us" and theirs is "old testament invigilator" we're never going to have a meaningful conversation. If our version of love is "mutual respect and co-creativity" and theirs is "marriage contract and compromise", same problem. If our version of work is "creative fulfillment" and theirs is "discipline and responsibility" ditto.

The other problem with rebellion is that we layer our newfound creative impulse on top of old-fashioned foundation stones, so the new structures we build are often a bit unstable. We find out how unstable when we go home.

It often goes a little like this:

We engage in polite conversation. We run out of things to say. We swerve into the territory of our particular brand – our worldview. Things get heated. There is a "brand stand off", followed by silence. As always we are trying to deal with this with our mind rather than our heart. We get crazy because we want to inflict our worldview on them, but they have an entirely different context. Their context is "hard work and obedience to the rules." This applies to their spiritual life, their married life and their work life. If we come along with "Neither God, your boss or your spouse want or appreciate your sacrifices, they want you to be creative and happy" this isn't going to encourage them to change their brand.

Then of course there's the inevitability of projection – "Will I be like this in years to come?" It's easy to be brave when nothing threatens us, but will we be as plucky when we face the fear and insecurity of old age.

I am sitting in my father's house, surrounded by framed photographs of the past, wondering how long I can keep my heart open while my body reacts? I'm aiming for five minutes. It's tougher than you think. I remember Chloe doing the "chair" exercise, but now I'm in the real chair without a safety net. I don't have the distance of visualization. I'm face to face with the real thing.

It's difficult being with what is when it changes so dramatically from what was. My father was my first Apollo projection. Godlike, magnificent, charismatic, generous, quick to anger. Winning his approval was like basking in the glow of a super trouper. Now he is old and trying to cope with diminishing faculties. He is fighting against the dimming of the light. It's what our left-brain loves to do - rage and rally. The quieter voice of our right-brain is calling for us to surrender into the beauty of a different kind of light. The left thinks "surrender" sounds a lot like "giving up" and advocates a strategy involving medicines, vitamin supplements and brainteasers.

We assess our age by comparing it to the things we can still do rather than our capacity to fully inhabit the space where we are now. We say things like "I have the lungs of a 30 year old" to demonstrate our fitness level. We glow with pride when people say we look "young for our age." We have become a nation obsessed with youth. We don't even want to look at old people in case it reminds us of our mortality. This is wishful thinking gone mad or in other words, delusion.

While my father fights, my stepmother copes. They are both being heroic according to some handed down tradition. It is the type of heroism that made generations of people work hard, fight wars and make personal sacrifices. These things are neither good nor bad... as always it's the energy driving them that determines their value. A life of hard work and service can be a wonderful thing, if done with grace, i.e. with no expectation (one glimpse of the radiant face of Mother Theresa proves that the bliss of living in that type of grace, is its own reward).

Unfortunately most of us are engaged in the counterfeit ego version – hard work to compensate for our lack of self worth, and sacrifice to pay off our imagined guilt. It's a vicious circle. We feel bad. We work hard. We feel good, and then we feel exhausted. We seek release in complaining and resentment. This causes us to feel bad. To relieve the guilt, we work hard. Then we feel exhausted... and so it goes.

My father and stepmother are really good people. They both worked hard all their lives. They have always done the right thing. Neither of them are in their right mind. It is heartbreaking to watch. We think retirement will bring a respite from hard work, but because most of the work is going on in our head, this is not the case. With greater access to the right-brain we could work much harder and not feel tired at all. We could be driven by grace. Grace is a very high-octane fuel, extremely effective and creates no wear and tear on the engine.

The ego hates grace and convinces us that suffering is much more noble. It persuades us that we have committed some awful crime for which we have to feel bad. None of us is immune to this particular spell. We hide the guilt of our imagined crimes with purposefulness. If we want to mooch about in a dressing gown all morning and the postman calls we say "I've just got out of the shower" to hide our obviously slothful nature. If we want to go on holiday we feel we have to justify it with claims that we are "exhausted" so need a holiday because we have been "working so hard." It's nonsense. Who are we trying to fool, apart from ourselves? No one else cares. We cover up our imagined flaws with what looks like a lot of action, but it's coming from the wrong place, so all our hard work is a contrivance.

I drink tea and listen to the extended news on TV. It's something I never do in my own house (the headlines are bad enough). The gratuitous attention to detail just adds to the doom and gloom. Old people shouldn't listen to the news. It's no wonder they're frightened of the world. Yet, because of their free time, they seem to listen to the news more than anybody. Chloe's grandmother phones her on a regular basis just to check she is still alive. She thinks life in London is something along the lines of Grand Theft Auto.

Eventually it is time to leave. My heart feels heavy but I am determined to do something different. I hold my father's hand, look into his eyes and let go of any need to change his mind. Instead I choose to love him in this moment, which is the only moment there is. He looks momentarily embarrassed, but to my surprise he doesn't look away. I feel a release of energy in my heart and he smiles. It is a short moment in time but a profound one in space. There is a shift of energy, from changing his mind to changing my heart. Unconditional love trumps rebellion. Something new has entered the space created. As I let go of his hand, my whole being is suffused with an exquisite feeling.

It is grace.

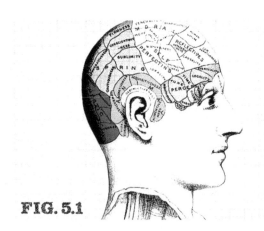

FIG. 5.1

Crowded House

DAY THIRTY FIVE

Driving home, I pass the cemetery where my mother has been for over two thirds of my life. I try to remember her. The only feelings I can conjure up are less than helpful. There was the funeral itself during which time my damsel was in her element. I was so busy identifying with the personification of grief that I forgot to grieve. My focus was on the drama, the dress (black) and the demeanor (tragic). After the event a much worse feeling came... guilt. I was a heartless, horrid, attention-seeking daughter who deserved to be cursed. Knowing that guilt is not a real emotion, I pulled the car into the side of the road and sat with the feeling.

Under the guilt was something worse. Dissociation.

I couldn't get beneath the dissociation. The superglue of guilt had welded it down. I couldn't feel anything. How can I release something I can't feel? I need to go back to the Greeks for guidance.

It's easy to think that the male Gods had all the best lines. Compared to the high drama in the skies, the earth has a more static beauty. Male gods have great mobility so they can blow up a storm or impregnate things. Female goddesses nurture the planted seeds. They are profoundly affected by the seasons and if they are loved enough, they can maintain their beauty throughout all of them.

In our modern, youth obsessed world, older women are not celebrated. This is a problem for many reasons, and not just the obvious one that wise women are an incredibly creative resource. If a culture associates power with youth, then as soon as men reach the peak of their earthly powers there is an assumption that they will reward themselves with a younger wife. This is terrifying for the female goddesses. They give up on the job they are supposed to do (protecting the earth for the good of everybody) and instead they spend an enormous amount of energy trying to fight the autumn and winter of their years.

Entirely new industries geared to support this fear have exploded on the planet - plastic surgery, botox, and liposuction. Women have lost their way. Their concept of beauty has been distorted, and little wonder - the fear has been gathering energy since the ancient Greeks! A woman who is loved by a man in her later years, becomes a powerful force of nature. In order for this to happen she has to learn to trust. It is very difficult for a man to love an angry woman. In order to trust, she has to break the spells of thousands of years.

The union between a man and a woman has the kind of power that frightens us. In the spring and summer of our years we can dilute the power of this union by having children. This is natural but has some traps that need to be avoided. The first trap is that women turn away from their mate, and fall in love with their children. This allows them to experience a much safer version of power. There is no opposing force (until teenage years and even that is pretty tame.) Women can become so comfortable with this union that they forget that it was supposed to be temporary in nature. Then of course, in the autumn and winter of our years, fear of ageing consumes our power. Neither of these two pulls on our energy can ever have a happy outcome. Children becoming adults and women becoming old are inevitable. It's time to get through these surface fears and tackle the major league fear beneath both of them.

Again it's intimacy. Not the intimacy between man and woman, though this is a great portal - intimacy between ourselves and the "all is one." Instead of moving in this direction we create a left-brain strategy for the female life cycle as follows:

We emerge into adulthood and become mesmerized by the outside world. First through the mirror (of our narcissism.) Then by Narcissus himself (our chosen Prince.) Then by our children (how fabulous.) Then by the mirror again (this time, think Snow White's stepmother.) Finally by Estee Lauder (just kidding.)

A better right-brain strategy would be the following:

We emerge into adulthood and become mesmerized by the outside world. First through the mirror (narcissism.) Then by Narcissus (Prince.) Then by our children (within reason.) Then we go back to Narcissus (having evolved to King.) We form a true partnership, buy soft focus mirrors, and grow old gracefully (i.e. filled with grace.) The grace enables us to engage in high-level creativity and tantric sex (for the good of humanity.)

Outcome: Intimacy with the "all is one."

No. 35 Queen lyrics fit for a King 'Thunderbolt and lightning very, very frightening…. me'

Time for some Greek mythology. If we want to further pursue the original pattern of our fear of intimacy we need to visit the underworld via the story of Demeter and Persephone.

Demeter was Goddess of Fertility and all things that grew from the earth. She looked after the cycles of nature, made sure the corn ripened and that all the humans and animals were fed. She mated with Zeus and they had a daughter called Persephone who became the maiden High Priestess. Persephone was the original hippy child, loved, happy and innocent. One day, while she was wandering the fields picking wild flowers and no doubt singing folk songs, she was spotted by Hades. Hades was looking for a wife and asked Zeus if he could have Persephone. Zeus saw no problem with this, but said Demeter would never agree, so advised Hades to kidnap her. (It was the kind of unsophisticated strategy Zeus had used in the past to great effect.)

Hades emerged from the underground on a black chariot, probably the ancient Greek equivalent to a red Ferrari, and abducted Persephone. Demeter searched high and low and couldn't find her anywhere. She was completely grief stricken. More than this she just wouldn't give up (let's hear it for the tenacity of Mothers!) Zeus was surprised by this (he probably thought it would all blow over.) During one of those quiet awful moments, he finally admitted that Persephone was down in the underworld and that he sort of sanctioned it. Demeter was FURIOUS and went into complete despair during which time everything stopped growing. The earth became barren. It was like the nuclear winter of malcontent. All the humans and animals began to starve.

There are a few things to know about the Underworld. First, it is harder to get into than a Led Zeppelin gig, and it's even harder to leave. It is surrounded by the River Styx and patrolled by Cerberus, a three-headed dog who kills all trespassers. Once you manage to get past security, if you eat ANYTHING at all you can NEVER leave. The only God who can get in and out of the Underworld is Hermes - I think immigration are just mesmerized by the quality of his accessories. Demeter negotiated a deal with Hermes and asked him to go and get her daughter back.

Meanwhile, back in the underworld, as soon as Hades installed Persephone in her new home, he offered her food. At first she refused (she'd heard the rumors) but eventually she ate some pomegranate seeds – (being a hippy child she probably thought these would help with the free radicals.) By the time Hermes arrived her fate was sealed - she could never leave. Demeter was now insane with grief and rage. Zeus was in BIG trouble.

In order for life to carry on (remember nothing was growing and the humans and animals were starving) a special deal was worked out between Hades, Zeus and the Three Fates. Persephone was allowed to go back to her mother but had to return to the underworld for several months, every year... forever. (During which time Demeter goes back into mourning.) This is the season of winter, when everything stops growing. Spring heralds the return of Persephone to her mother. We've been having longer winters lately. Persephone seems reluctant to return home - perhaps she's having too much fun in the underworld. In fact this story is also about sex and the need for daughters to separate from their mothers, so that they can experience their own sexuality. It's also about letting go - something Demeter is clearly not very good at.

So, back to the present moment. Where am I in this story? I have successfully let go of my own children. But I didn't have a chance to separate gracefully from my mother. Mothers represent the feminine side of our nature. If there are problems here, there will definitely be problems with creativity. I need a Hermes to go rescue her from the other side. Then I need to do a deal with the Fates. Scrolling through the contacts on my phone I know just the man for the job. Coach and former pirate... Jeff Allen.

Mama told me not to come... (Three headed dog night)

DAY THIRTY SIX

Pop lyrics No. 36 It's different for Girls... Joe Jackson

I wake up to wild stormy weather. If I listened to the news it would probably be full of commuting drama – trains not running due to an abundance of leaves blown onto tracks, trees falling down and blocking side roads, flooding in coastal areas. Weather like this could make you believe in angry male Gods. Fortunately I have never been near a tsunami, an earthquake or a volcano erupting – these stirrings from Mother Nature in the depths below, are always more destructive. It's no wonder we have such a fear of the unconscious female world.

On my way over to Jeff's house, I ponder my journey so far. I've been relentless in my search for the "stuck" unfelt feelings in my energy system. I've visited the neediness of the damsel and the guilt of the child. I've experienced the rebellious tantrum against my father. What is there left to feel? What is underneath the dissociation between me and my mother?

I think about all the judgments I have on women. I know this is the first question he'll ask me. The first thing we do if we're afraid of something is to separate ourselves from it so that we can keep it in the external world where we can heap scorn on it. The greater the judgment, the greater the fear and the greater the need for distance. Another vicious circle. The left-brain loves patterns but it loves circular patterns most of all.

Jeff greets me at the door and leads me to the inner sanctum. I sit and reel off my judgments. I think women are mad, hysterical, manipulative, devious and needy. That sums up into a pretty damning trilogy - crazy, pathetic and not to be trusted. I know there's good stuff too but right now I'm trying to consolidate my deepest, darkest beliefs. Jeff smiles.

First he encourages me to take my focus away from the form and put it onto the energy. If we want to make sense of the unconscious world we need to get away from our tendency to turn everything into form. The left-brain obviously loves form because it helps with the pattern recognition. Jeff steers me in the direction of the right-brain where everything is about the energy that drives the form.

This is easier because it takes the judgment off all those mad queens, vampires, wicked stepmothers and needy damsels and it places it onto the energy of chaos - how the energy is before it takes form. We all have masculine and feminine energy. Men distance themselves from their feminine energy and women define themselves by theirs. That's why they hate themselves so much. Remember Narcissus was male – if he'd been female, the myth would have collapsed. A woman would have looked into the pond and immediately started criticizing the size of her nose, wailed at the condition of her skin, and far from being transfixed and unable to move she would have rushed off to find a decent hairbrush.

Feminine energy, like nuclear energy, is a source of power wrapped up in our greatest fear. It looks like the kind of chaos that our left-brain is incapable of controlling. That's why we continually hit the circuit breaker. We have to learn to be with the things we can't control. If we engage with the physical world without reacting or dissociating, we can begin to occupy the space between worlds.

Jeff makes a cup of tea. He's done this journey before me. He has in fact sailed single handedly across the globe. It was tough but not as tough as getting other people to make a decision. Independent people like to control things on their own and they're strong enough to do it - for a while. One day, in a damascene moment, his life changed forever. He stood on the brow of a ship, stared out to the horizon and realized he could not remember the last time he had felt truly happy.

Jeff would not be sitting in the relationship guru seat if he hadn't made the long journey across both desert and sea to the epi center.

We talk about the way I could not feel anything during my mother's funeral. I realize that this was because I didn't lose my mother when her body left the physical plane. Energetically I lost her way before that, when I was a very young child. Many of us do. Like many mothers of her generation she was floundering and powerless. She was married to Apollo, with no voice of her own. She was incredibly creative, with no possibility of creative expression other than child bearing and husband supporting. She had a mystical connection to a world that was hurting, with no power to help the suffering she had such empathy for. She could feel everything, but she could do nothing about it.

Like many "good mothers" she did not express this as rage, she contained the energy by turning it inwards. She swallowed a nuclear reactor. It's a wonder she didn't implode earlier.

I am starting to feel slightly unhinged. I allowed this to happen. Far from supporting her in her distress, I distanced myself as quickly as possible and formed a bond with my father. He seemed more powerful. I didn't want all that chaos, I wanted something solid. Like a piece of electricity finding an earthing rod, I ran to him and clung on for dear life. It looked ok to the outside world. Daddy's girl became the tomboy, who went on to become the successful businesswoman. But as I revisit the early scene of the crime, with Hermes by my side, I start to feel a powerful feeling. It is strong enough to push through the disassociation.

It is betrayal.

The bible has many powerful stories, mostly revolving around men. Men rewrote the stories of Jesus hundreds of years after his death and all female roles were heavily edited, in fact only two female roles remained – the mother and the prostitute. One of the most popular biblical stories is The Prodigal Son. In this tale a father has two sons. One is the "good son" who does everything right. One is the "black sheep" who squanders his inheritance on wine, women and song. Eventually, flat broke, the black sheep shuffles back to his father. He is expecting the hiding of his life but his Dad is so happy at his return, that he throws a huge banquet in his honor.

This story is interesting for two reasons. First it shows that the source of supreme creativity (the father) doesn't care how bad we've been, but just wants us to rejoin the family (the whole of humanity.) The source is proud when we "have a go" at creativity. The second reason the story is interesting is that there is no female equivalent in the bible – obviously all references to the feminine were left on the cutting room floor. In the interests of karmic balance, I will include one here.

The Return of the Prodigal Daughter.

A mother has two daughters. One does everything right, the other runs away to join the boys club and live a life of independence.

Eventually the black sheep, exhausted from insomnia and desperate to finish the book she is trying to write, turns up at the house of Hermes. (She has lost the way back to her mother's house and needs help). She is also frightened. (Like the prodigal son she is expecting the hiding of her life). Hermes takes her by the hand and leads her to the portal of feminine energy.

I am now still sitting opposite Jeff, determined to stay with the feeling of betrayal I am experiencing. The feeling morphs and weaves through shame, guilt and regret. Eventually what breaks through is so painful that I understand the expression "being brought to your knees." It is a wave of pain from beyond the periphery of my personal "self", perhaps from a time before that boundary was even established. It seems to encompass all the lost and abused children of the world, their heartbreak, loneliness and fear. It's the pain my mother carried. The force of the wave crashes through all barriers like a tsunami. Finally I can experience and name the feeling I've defended myself against for most of my life.

Devastation.

I can hear Jeff mumbling something in the background. He is encouraging me to breathe. I know why the dissociation was so firmly welded. I am helpless to survive. The only option is to surrender. Death seems preferable. As I feel myself drowning, my lungs screaming for release, I breathe in.

Peace comes first. Stillness. Quiet. Wonder. What follows is indescribable beauty. It is the energy of unconditional love. I have rescued my mother. And in so doing I have rescued myself.

Black hole – instant death or portal to another dimension?

DAY THIRTY SEVEN

David Bowie lyrics No. 37 **"I look at my watch it says 9.25 and I think Oh God I'm still alive"**

I had no idea how long I spent at Jeff's before I got in my car to leave. Time is a funny construct when you slip over the other side of it. Waiting for the energy can be a bit like sitting in a boat, wondering where the tornado is going to hit. There are various clues that you could pursue, but these can be ego traps that just take you off in the wrong direction. It takes an experienced tracker to guide you to the perfect storm. Particularly as it's the last place the ego wants to sail into.

I feel different. Not different in a "seen the light" sort of way. No donkeys were harmed during this transformation process. I don't want to leap about shouting hallelujah like a born again Christian - or even murmur it Leonard Cohen style. I feel very still inside. For once my mind is quiet and there is no emotion in the pit of my stomach. A profound shift seems to have taken place. This is what spiritual alchemy is about. The changing of matter to energy and the changing of energy to matter.

It all makes sense to me in retrospect. I remember when my twin daughters were babies. If one of them started crying, the other would start up straight away. Later on I found this was called "empathic distress". In other words, babies, not yet having a sense of identity automatically feel all pain as their own. As the "self" develops and we realize we are separate from others, this wiring allows us to have empathy. We can "put ourselves in another's shoes" and imagine how they feel. You could say this is the "Intel inside" that would ensure the survival of our species. We're actually wired for sociability and compassion, not competition and aggression. But first we have to disable the firewall.

The reason we're frightened of removing this shield is because we are connected to the "all that is" - the sum total of human experience, with its joys and genius, its injustice and pain. We think if we were to feel that much it would break our heart.

In fact it just breaks the shield. Our hearts can't break because they're connected to all that is.

When the shield is dismantled, new, different energy can come in. This new energy, untainted by the belief systems of the past is full of possibilities. It's important not to look back at this point. With just one thought we can start to rebuild the old template. This is why Jesus advised the people he healed not to go back to their villages for a little while. The desire to show off the new template and say "Look I can walk!" or "Look I'm cool with chaos" can have disastrous effects. One cynical response to our newfound freedom, one moment of self-doubt, can start a whole chain reaction, and before we know it we've reconstructed the pattern all over again. Remember Lot's wife - don't look back! Stay in the present!

The present moment is brilliant because it knows nothing about the past. It's always a brand new start, every second. The Greeks had their own word for the "now" moment. Kairos. They had two forms of time: Chronos time (we call it chronological but it's the same thing) covers events that happen in linear sequence, i.e. one after the other. Kairos time is the serendipitous "magical" time that occurs when we unite with the source of supreme creativity to create something fabulous. This is when time (Chronos version) stands still.

Needless to say, all creativity happens in Kairos time. If we want to be creative we have to ditch our fascination with Chronos – get rid of the old story, forget where it all went wrong in the past, forgive everyone (including ourselves!) and move on. We need to stop looking at photographs of how great, slim and cute we used to be (Chronos time) and we need to forge a new relationship with Kairos, where the party is happening all the time... now.

The world of Kairos has rules. It requires that we show up and "Be present". There must be a hundred small ways we can learn how to "be" in the new creative world. First we have to stop all our displacement activity! No more standing in an elevator staring at our shoes, or sitting at a party checking our blackberry - we only create this distance to ease our discomfort. No more fighting at work or sulking at home - we create these dramas to fill the silence. If we develop the courage to feel, we can just "be" with any and all feelings that arise and we could also "be" with the absence of any activity (the void of possibility which is the crucible for new energy.)

I think about my Dad again. It's probably too late to change his relationship to time and space. Older people have lots of time, but they still manage to fill it with constant mental activity. When I went home I offered to take him out for lunch. He was ready to go shortly after breakfast. I've been guilty of this tendency to usher in the next moment too soon, rather than just "being with" whatever is. Now I'm practicing being with those intervening moments - the quiet empty ones that are pregnant with possibility.

I wish my father could unhook himself from the five sensory world he controls so fervently, and allow himself to fall into the vastness of the different dimensions that exist beyond the fear. But I can't change his reality and I'm ok with that. Not long ago I thought his ability to be in control was powerful; now I know my mother was powerful beyond measure - she just didn't know it.

If we want to be impregnated with the source of supreme creativity, we have to be courageous enough to stand in the empty crucible of the void. As Eckhart Tolle says "live in the power of now." Or, as Jesus says, "seek first the kingdom" - get into Kairos time, then hold on... I'm coming. (Actually this was Sam and Dave but they were probably in Kairos when they wrote it.)

To perform spiritual alchemy, there are two things we have to become comfortable with - stillness and emotion. Our mind is uncomfortable with both... it seeks to fill the stillness and control the emotion. This is where we need our heart.

Emotion is an incredibly powerful force. In order to be effective in the world – i.e. give creative expression to the things we love or create solutions for the things we don't, we have to use the intelligence of the heart (and yes, the heart does have its own intelligence.) For the past few hundred years we have relied solely on the intelligence of the mind, but scientists now have proof that the heart is 5000 times stronger magnetically and 100 times stronger electrically, than the brain. As we live in an electro magnetic field, it makes sense to use the organ most appropriate for the terrain we inhabit.

Our old system is broken. We need a different system for our new creative world. What would this look like?

A different relationship to time – living in the "Now" moment, without fear of the future or nostalgia for the past. Allowing what wants to emerge.

A different relationship to space – actually "being" in the space we are in, without creating the diversions of distance and drama. Prepared to be seen, naked.

A different mind – clear of mental chatter; balanced between left and right-brain. With no need to fill the stillness.

A different heart – clear of unexploded bombs; open and available to feel. With no need to control the emotions.

A different body – finely tuned to the five senses plus the intuitive hits of the sixth.

Almost an entirely different human being! Certainly one that is capable of channeling high voltage creative energy. It's time to surrender the old operating system and embrace the new upgrade.

Perhaps the book I was writing will fall away, to be replaced by a different one. Perhaps this is the book I am writing. Surrender is a powerful concept. It's not the white flag of giving up. It's the colorful flare that indicates we are ready to begin...

Salvador Dali's concept of time. He lived in Kairos - what can I say!

DAY THIRTY EIGHT

Song lyric No. 38 "Into the mystic" **The skinny on the true feminine**

I am almost at the end of the forty days. Chloe is sitting opposite me in the kitchen where it all began, having a cup of tea and a piece of cake. She is texting one of my daughters with relationship advice. She wants some good to come from the extensive field research she has carried out on "the love of narcissistic men." The beginning of her TV drama is hilarious so this is an added bonus.

My other daughter has been rehearsing for her end of term musical *Wicked*. She is singing *Defy Gravity*, which is an appropriate metaphor to describe the journey we are all on. In our ascent to the higher planes of creativity, we have to defy the magnetic pull of lower consciousness.

We are three generations of women "in transition" - a creative trinity! My daughters are leaving childhood behind as they experience life away from home for the first time. Chloe is transforming from "damsel" to "woman in charge of her own destiny" as she chooses a healthier outlet for all her creative energy. I am embracing the wise woman, as I prepare to step into a true partnership with Apollo.

Transitions are always a difficult time in the world of archetypes. Some of the stronger ones are reluctant to leave the stage to make way for the new.

During transits it is even more important to become comfortable with Kairos time. First, because we need to be aware of serendipitous signs, and clues that point us in the new direction. Second, because we sometimes have to be patient with what wants to emerge. Our ego fights with us on this one, because it doesn't have the patterning in place for the new archetype. The trap we usually fall into is "Show me the pattern, then I'll step into it." The non-physical world (where there is no fear) says, "Trust what isn't there yet. Take a step. Then the new pattern will emerge – the GPS won't work unless you're moving."

Creativity requires that we rediscover how to think like a child. In other words we have to re-learn how to trust and how to play with imaginary friends. If this sounds bonkers to us we must remember the way Steve Jobs turned Apple into the most successful company on the planet. He didn't do it by asking his customers what they wanted or by investing in focus groups, analysis and market research. He observed that "customers can't visualize what doesn't exist, so they don't know what they want." Luckily Steve could visualize. He knew how to co-create with the energy, how to make friends with what isn't here yet. It was the death knell for the left-brainers.

This is the grown up, mystical interpretation of "become like little children."

From a holistic point of view, as a species, we are all at this point. We're standing on the verge of the new paradigm. We urgently need to visualize a new and better way of doing just about everything. We need the vision for i-health, i-government, i-media, i-legislation and i-environment. Money is no longer a meaningful medium of exchange. Creativity is. Money doesn't represent value to us any more. Creativity does.

If we synchronize our watches to Kairos time and move forward, a new channel of creativity will open up for us. As we learn how to read the energy of what is emerging from collective consciousness, we can join in. Life is more enjoyable when we participate. We have clues about which direction the energy is moving in. Anodea Judith describes this pattern brilliantly in the four ages, as follows...

At the beginning of Chronos time, the world was dominated by static feminine energy. Early humans lived in harmony with nature. We glorified birth and fertility. This was the time of agriculture. There was peace - but not a whole lot going on.

Next came dynamic masculine energy. As the name implies we became vigorous and focused and created fantastic things to make our lives better. This was the time of industry – engineering, architecture and science. We also became highly competitive, which led to a lot of aggression and fighting.

The world couldn't sustain this drama for too long so it was time for another shift. The logical choice would have been to flip back to the feminine for a few hundred years but the masculine energy didn't want to give up its supremacy, so the shift that occurred was from dynamic masculine to static masculine, where we are now.

During this static masculine age, a lot of the good aspects of masculine energy became codified and stuck. Static masculine, as its name suggests, is all about defending the territory won, the money made and the status achieved via wars, legislation, and command and control behaviors. Common sense and compassion took a back seat. Our ability to trust, to receive inspiration and to co-create with the energy that wants to emerge was well and truly lost.

We stand on the brink of a new era - the fourth part of the square. The missing piece is the dynamic feminine. This is something we have no template for yet and precious few role models. It is not the feminine portrayed by victims, femme fatales, violent queens or naïve innocents. It is not gender specific (sorry girls, there'll be no "They messed up, now it's our turn.") We wouldn't have done any better. There are numerous examples of women who got their hands on power and did a pretty good version of the bully archetype.

This new era is not about gender; it's about the correct use of creative power. Instead of learning how and where to throw thunderbolts (very masculine) we have to learn how to become better vessels of creative energy (receiving is a feminine thing). In this way we can channel the power more wisely.

Welcoming back the lost feminine is the story of the prodigal daughter. We all have a sense of being orphaned. It's a universal feeling. We're motherless children who have become feral and destructive to the planet. We've squandered our inheritance. The prodigal son's inheritance was one of the mind, the prodigal daughter's is one of the heart. When people lose heart, they lose the will to live and hence we have a global epidemic in depression. But the other reason for winning our heart back is because that's where the power is. That's where passion resides. Feelings are more powerful than thoughts.

So back to "archetypes in transition." On a personal level, how do we move from a life pattern that is no longer fulfilling us to a different one? On a global level, how do we move from the structures we have created (financial, political, media) to better versions of the same – versions that would ensure we don't destroy ourselves?

In all mythologies, the hero always has to pass a test before new power can be conferred onto him. His heart and mind have to be challenged to make sure he is up to the task. Before our new (waiting in the wings) archetypes emerge, we have to face the challenge of the four horsemen of the apocalypse. Just kidding (but equally grim), we have to face the four archetypes of survival. Remember these guys? Before we step up to the new level, we will come face to face with these four sentries.

The child, victim, prostitute and saboteur are ruthless circuit breakers of power. In order to neutralize these parts of our nature, we have to be prepared to rise to the challenge each one poses.

Our child has to overcome the need to be indulged and the fear of making a mistake. Then it can become magical.

Our victim has to overcome the default pattern for getting our needs met via drama. Then it can become victorious.

Our prostitute has to overcome the tendency to negotiate our creativity in exchange for money. Then it can become the lover.

Our saboteur has to overcome the fear of power itself and the million excuses we use to sabotage it or slow it down. Then it can become creative.

The child and victim are archetypes based on need and the prostitute and saboteur archetypes are based on control. As we have seen we tend to associate more with the controlling ones and project the needy ones onto the people around us, but both sides are equally destructive on an unconscious level. Once we are aware of the patterns, we can co-exist peacefully with each of them while working on their evolution.

"Working" is the key word! We don't just acknowledge our inner child, victim, prostitute or saboteur while indulging their behaviors because they are "understandable" patterns. This gives us a reason to stay stuck, not a solution for the stickiness. We are living in a new era with complex challenges and these old survival behaviors hinder rather than help us survive. We need to evolve the patterns so there isn't so much resistant energy around, blocking the cool creative energy that wants to emerge.

Many years ago I worked as a tour manager for Van Morrison, funnily enough during the time he produced an album called *A Period of Transition* so this is an apposite story. The band line up featured Mo Foster on bass, Peter Van Hook on drums, Mick Ronson (of Ziggy

Stardust fame) on guitar, Dr John on keyboards and Van on vocals. The tour was chaos. Mo and Pete were long suffering in the face of conflicting egos spinning at different speeds. Mick Ronson was taking amphetamines and doing everything at a hundred miles an hour. Dr John was on methadone and doing everything very, very slowly. Van was bouncing around in the middle.

Thinking back, it's easy to see how something with the potential to be magnificent could go so wrong. This was in the pre-rap days when the closest musicians came to improvisation was the ubiquitous guitar solo. A few drummers tried, but (with the exception of Ginger Baker) no one managed to pull it off. Singers didn't improvise, unless they were back up, when they were allowed a little creative freedom with the shoop shoops and the bee baps.

Apart from Van Morrison.

He could stand at a microphone, close his eyes and out of his mouth would come the most amazing lyrics, completely improvised. Later on, when Rolling Stone journalists would analyze and dissect the lyrical poetry, he became cross and grumpy. They were using the left-brain to discuss the song writing techniques he employed, or to discover the etymology of the words he used. Van didn't have a left-brain. That's why he wrote such great songs. This made for some very interesting, and increasingly short conversations.

Van was managed by Harvey Goldsmith at the time. When he pre-planned the tour, it looked like a great combination of musicians. Unfortunately, as soon as the team got on the road, the four survival archetypes took over. Child (Mick Ronson) Victim (Dr John) Prostitute (Mo 'n Pete) and Saboteur (Van). Now there were some crazy people on the tour bus and it was just a matter of time before the bomb got detonated. Harvey's response was to try to control the situation. As we've noticed in our own lives, we can't control an electro magnetic field without disastrous results.

We all have each one of these four survival archetypes. We have to own them and have some serious grown up conversations before we allow them on the bus. We also need to birth some new archetypes for the times we live in, ones that operate under the principles of the dynamic feminine. The chaos (that the right-brain is connected to) does not respond to rules, but it adapts well to principles – principles have the right amount of flexibility.

Life ultimately is about the management of power. If we want a more creative life, we need to take a look at the various ways we've been managing it so far, and make some improvements. Rather than using discipline to make ourselves more creative, we need to use discipline to increase our receptivity and our ability to trust.

High-level creativity isn't something we do; it's something we receive.

High-level creativity isn't about pursuing the answers; it's about falling in love with the questions, falling in love with the mystery of life.

The feminine archetype that wants to emerge in this new era is the Mystic. (Not the personality of the mystic, I hasten to add - please save us from the new age version of flowing robes, trinkets, aphorisms and bad website design.)

The Mystic is about "Being in love with being."

Because it is in service to the source of supreme creativity, the mystic is both intuitive and inclusive. It is feminine - in its true sense of the word.

I wonder what Apollo will make of her?

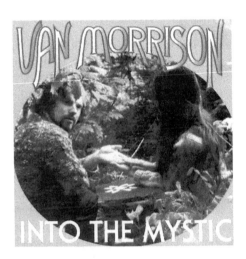

Van - the man (though curious absence of left-brain dominance)

DAY THIRTY NINE

Movie title No. 39 "True Grit" The skinny on the true masculine

Long email this morning from Apollo. He is just finishing off his work in Nigeria and will be home in a couple of days. He has endured an exhausting cocktail of third world travel - from the lack of Internet, hot running water and recognizable food to the surfeit of gunpoint security checks causing 30 mile tailbacks over which thousands of hawkers and ragamuffins scurry, in their attempts to eek out a modest existence.

Against this backdrop he is working on strategies to deal with the complex problems caused by business and political corruption, poverty and overcrowding. Rather than feeling hopelessly depressed, Apollo is eternally optimistic. Instead of witnessing the chaotic, broken systems on the surface, he sees evidence of living emergent systems that just need a little finessing to become sustainable.

Having written about the dynamic feminine perhaps its time to say something about its true counterpart... the dynamic masculine. After all, the world won't be saved until there is unity between the two. All our previous wrong turns and blind alleys seem to come from pendulum swings. We go from the politics of the right to the politics of the left and back to the right when we see the unwanted consequences. We hate the control of the right, and then we hate the dependency of the left.

Both behaviors are equally flawed and make us long for a return to more dynamic times when John Wayne was sheriff and people could get some sleep at night. It's tempting to think that it's not the system that's wrong; we're just lacking some real heroes. This is of course true, but has been interpreted by the ego in less than helpful ways...

Our modern day heroes are celebrities who owe much of their status to the spinning wheels of PR companies. At any moment they could prick their finger and fall into a deep sleep of obscurity. Because of this, they feel vulnerable rather than heroic. The PR machine can be turned onto anybody - as long as fame is their primary objective. Now we don't know how to make heroes out of real people.

A new hero for our times would have all the energy and certainty of John Wayne with all the love and wisdom of the mystic. What would this look like? Strangely enough, rather like a boy child - curious, creative, brimming with energy and full of love.

All children have a gifted spirit, but boys in particular have a tendency to associate with the hero. When they play, they will always identify with the toy that "helps" - the train engine that rescues, the bunny rabbit that saves the day or solves the problem. The spirit part of them has the instinct to know that part of their destiny is to help others. It knows that the "happy ever after" ending can't come about until everybody wins in some way. Their spirit (being eternal) feels invincible, resourceful and creative. Their body (being only a few years old) becomes stressed by the enormity of the task at hand. As they move towards the emotional pain in the family, they get stuck, and then they construct a belief that they have failed.

This feeling of failure is so crushing that they have to disconnect from their hearts. Because of their task-oriented disposition, the disconnection happens earlier than it does for girls - which is why they often find it so much more difficult to trace their way back. I remember the games my children used to play when they were small... my daughters wanted to love (everything from dolls to small rodents), but my son wanted to help – that was how he expressed his love.

Grown up boys are right now either rushing around the office, trying to solve problems... or flying around the globe, trying to save the world. A lot of this activity, though well meaning, is ineffective. Remember it's the energy driving the intention that creates the result. Much of this energy comes from the fear of failure, the shame of defeat and the desire to "do it right this time." If they could only break the shield over their hearts, they could re-connect to the energy of love. Then the new hero would emerge... the quintessential hero for our times. This has in fact already started to happen. (Tom Shadyac we salute you!)

In the meantime, we are bombarded with 24/7 media coverage of people who want to be famous for being famous, who want to be celebrated for the identity they have created. This strange diet has fed a generation who list "fame" as an aspiration. As a species, many people are not interested in changing the world – they think it's too complicated, and they don't trust any of its leaders. They are merely interested in *looking* cool, sincere, and concerned - not *being* any of these things. This is because they are not connected to their inner creative spirit.

We may think the Greek myths are ridiculous but imagine what future generations would say about our current beliefs. We have turned our self-hatred not into self-love but into self-obsession. We spurn reality but remain fascinated by reality television. Our heroes aren't lauded for changing the world; they are rewarded for changing their brand of clothing/shampoo/luggage. We have built huge systems to cover our mountain of debt. There is a smokescreen hiding our lack of direction and our castles are made of sand.

In short, we are under a spell as powerful as any ancient Greek curse. We are disconnected from life itself and are living a form of virtual reality that we all pretend is real. We endure a small existence by the side of the pond. This smallness is an attack on our highest potential. It gives us an excuse to withdraw to a safe distance. We stop sharing ourselves with the world. We become mean.

It's time for the true hero to emerge. Not one person who we can project our greatness and our flaws onto, but the dynamic masculine lying dormant in each of us. If we remove our focus from other people – secretly begrudging their success, celebrating their downfall, or feeling relieved that we don't have to endure their humiliation – we can turn the focus inside and start discovering who we really are. This is not the personality we have created and fallen in love with. It is so much more.

We need to lead ourselves out of the desert and if we all start becoming more honest about our hidden agendas, then hopefully this will take less than forty years. There's no room for any more politically correct, cosmetically enhanced leaders. We don't buy that any more. In the 1960s three in four people trusted political leaders, now that figure is one in four. We don't need our leaders to be nice; we need them to be real.

The symbolic meaning behind the yearning involved in the story of Narcissus and his unrequited love is the loss of connection to our soul. Our soul has a destiny to fulfill and with time in short supply, it is desperate for us to wake up from the spell we are under. That destiny has something to do with helping humanity survive as a species. It involves love. Its driving force is creativity. It involves creativity. Its driving force is love. Both are true. We need to tear ourselves away from the illusions we stare into, turn 180 degrees and walk towards "becoming more real."

As Apollo has found over in Nigeria, the millions who live in extreme conditions are actually surviving quite well. Unfailing optimism carries them through. Their systems may look like chaos to us, because we are comparing them to the structured, neat, codified ones that we are familiar with. We have forgotten how irrelevant the concept of "looking good" is to the source of supreme creativity. It's energy that matters. They have bundles of it. We are so exhausted we can barely get out of bed. Keeping up appearances creates nothing of value, and is as deadly as sleeping in wet concrete.

The renaissance of the dynamic masculine will transform the world for the better. Safely contained by the dynamic feminine it will be free to fly, create, build and inspire. Liberated from the constraints of competition with others to prove its worth, it will know its true value and will inspire and enhance the values in others. Healed from the heartbreak that lies underneath the aggression, it will bring true peace. Loved and respected, it will evolve into a thing of beauty - the paradox of powerful benevolence. This isn't the stereotype of the new age hippy; it's rugged and determined.

After all... it's grit that makes the pearl in the oyster.

The boss... rebel with a cause

DAY FORTY

All good love stories end with a wedding. Despite the statistics we want to believe in the endurance of love and the hope that this ritual brings. We defy logic for good reason - some deeper part of ourselves knows that unity is our natural state. But it is the marriage of our self to our soul that is the real requirement here, not the marriage of our self to our projections.

Self-help adage No. 40 Love yourself

We've heard it before but what exactly does this mean? So far, this has come to mean, "Indulge yourself" which is not really the same thing. For years our lives were dictated by the rules of society. Our parents were told to work hard, be obedient and do the "right" thing. We are told to think outside the box, be inspired and love ourselves. This self-love was supposed to be a counter balance to the self-sacrifice endured by previous generations. In reality we have gone from one side of the pendulum to the other and both are equally off center.

Self-sacrifice doesn't help anybody. No one has ever been inspired by long faces, eye rolling, dark moods or deep sighs. Work that gets completed through the energy of sacrifice tends to be unimaginative, dreary and unappreciated by its recipient. The accusation "but I did all this for you" tends to be met with "I'd rather you hadn't." Making sacrifices becomes so exhausting that we are bound to rush to the flip side of indulgence. "I worked so hard, I deserve to treat myself."

What is the truth at the center saying? We need to be honest now. "Actually, I did all this for myself - to make me look good and to make you feel guilty."

In order to understand what "love yourself" really means we need to discern what "love" means. Prince Charles once famously shot himself in the foot by saying of Princess Diana "Of course I love her... whatever love means." There was outrage about his supposed heartlessness, but this was one of his most interesting comments. Clearly love meant something different to Diana. It meant romance. To Charles, love probably meant a contract for the good of the family and the nation, in the same way many marriages in the east are arranged.

However, romantic love, though it seems spontaneous, is frequently no less of an "arranged" marriage, it's just that the arranging is done more unconsciously. A girl who lacks confidence will fall in love with a boy who is self assured. The unspoken contract is that he will act as a substitute father figure, guiding and protecting her. If he stops doing this she will perceive that he doesn't love her. Similarly if the girl goes back to college, develops self-esteem or lands a brilliant job, he will perceive that she doesn't love him. They will say they "fell out of love" but really they "broke the terms of the arrangement."

Even the word "marriage" suffers from our projections. We'd like it to mean "unity" (as in two become one.) For girls, it often means something entirely different. It means "Being Chosen" (the final fulfillment of the deeply encoded fairytale of the Prince with the glass slipper.) This is about being soooooo special for one day that the rest of life seems dreary by comparison. The beginning of the marriage really signifies the end of the quest. If the aim is to be chosen, where can you go from there - apart from downhill?

It's interesting to note that this myth also applies to our creativity. I don't want to drive my creativity out into the world, via the Internet, I want the fairy Godmother of some publishing house to come with her magic wand and "choose" me. I want her to turn up with the coach and horses and transform the PDF to a beautifully designed book cover and say, "you shall go to the Oprah."

Time for a new story for love and creativity.

What love has come to mean in the western world is "need." Instead of "I love you" we might as well say "I need you" or "I need you to reflect a better version of me than the one I currently believe in." Apparently, some Indian tribes do not have a word for love. The closest they come is "I know you" meaning I understand you or I know what makes you tick. This is a deeper concept, it's basically saying, "I see who you really are and I'm still here!"

Just as real love doesn't make demands, real "self-love" doesn't make sacrifices or create indulgences. To love the self in its true sense is to esteem the self, so we can manage our own power. It stands to reason that if we are giving a lot of energy to our victim pattern, the way we love another will be dramatic and over emotional; if we are allocating energy to the prostitute, the way we love another will be a negotiation of some sort; if we are continually taken over by our child, the way we love will be needy and demanding and if we default continuously to the saboteur we will always remain scared of achieving true intimacy. If we work on transforming these archetypes so that we can represent our own power more fully, the way we love others will be vastly different.

Honoring our creativity involves raising the bar and integrating some new archetypes more appropriate to the times we're living in. Representing the energy of the dynamic masculine will be the Quintessential Hero. Representing the energy of the dynamic feminine will be the Mystic.

This is a truly powerful partnership for the new paradigm. It celebrates the different qualities of both without competing for supremacy. It's a holistic dynamic duo, able to tackle complex problems. The Mystic loves, nurtures and inspires the highest potential of a situation. The Quintessential Hero responds, creates and fulfills the promise.

The partnership of the Hero and the Mystic will facilitate another marriage... the union of love with creativity.

Creativity:

I went on this 40 day journey to find my inner creativity. I used to think that creativity was inside and problems were outside. But the reverse is true. Problems and blocks are on the inside and creativity is all around us. By emptying ourselves, we achieve a kind of alchemy – not base metal to gold, more solid metal to hollow bell. Guess which one resonates the loudest! Guess which one will be heard by the source of supreme creativity!

Love:

I used to think that love was the reward for hard work. But love is about receiving – from the energy of love that surrounds us. This automatically results in giving, but this giving comes from overflow, rather than from lack. If we vibrate at an energetic level of love, we show up on the radar of the source of supreme love and we get back more than we could possibly imagine.

Love is a state of "being."

"Being" ultimately involves an awareness of ourselves as a creative force.

***

My Cassandra mask has now become a feature on my desk, reminding me of the spell I have been under for so much of my life. She is actually looking more liberated as the days pass. Apollo returns this evening. I can feel the usual flurry of anticipation and excitement but at the same time I feel unusually calm. I've let go of my ridiculous attempts to compete with him and become committed to a joint collaboration of some kind. I've stopped using my imagination for fantasy and started using it to imagine what we could achieve together. If he invented the structure and I choreographed the energy, we could create a dance that the source of supreme creativity would be proud of.

I haven't finished my book, but have come up with a new title - *The A to Z of Be*. (I decided *The Sextant* was a bit too masculine!)

I've changed my mind about what creativity means. I'm going to make it part of my whole life, rather than something precious that I indulge in to enhance my identity.

I believe in love more than ever, but I'm looking forward to developing a capacity for mystical love rather than indulging in the roller coaster of power dynamics.

I've cleared some energetic blocks, which is great for being in the flow. Creative energy and sexual energy move along the same channels so even if my book does not materialize I could become a mistress of tantric sex, which is not the worse thing in the world. How impressed would Apollo be about that! Of course now that I am becoming an evolved spiritual being I will have to stop being a praise junkie - but we have to take our journey one step at a time.

I'm happy. Creativity is a wonderful thing and a big part of our purpose but our overall purpose is to be happy. Creativity helps us to be happy because it creates an attitude of mind – one of curiosity and wonder and living in the uncertainty of the emergent moment as it happens. It is exhilarating and scary but it beats the boring formulaic repetition of the familiar.

I do have a better alignment between my head and my heart on a vertical axis and between my left-brain and right-brain on a horizontal one. Thinking is great, but you can't think your way to happiness. Ideas and concepts are wonderful, but love isn't an idea or a concept... it's a reality. It's the reality of who we are.

The drama of Narcissus is coming to the end of its run. We've had enough of the love affair with our identity. We want to be in love with the essential part of ourselves. We want to be part of, not separate from the experience of our life. We don't want to watch it any more; we want to be in it. If we join forces we can remind ourselves that we must *"Step away from the pond, there's nothing to see here!"*

We start with a 180-degree turn and then we begin to walk, away from the water's edge, through the desert, to the Promised Land. There may not be milk and honey but there will be laughter, tears, emotion, creativity, great music and love... perhaps even confetti. (You can take the girl out of rom com but you can't take the rom com out of the girl.)

My phone pings. Apollo has landed!

My boyfriend's back and there's gonna be trouble (watch out world)
Hey la, hey la, my boyfriend's back

APPENDIX TAKEAWAYS

Day 1. Creativity is allowing yourself to make mistakes

Start bold. Do something. Go somewhere. Change one thing. Get over your fear of making a mistake. Mistakes can often be converted into valuable experiences.

Day 2. All experiences are meaningful and meaningless

Very few things matter really. Stop trying to be right. Instead, commit to the liberation of your right-brain. Practice looking at things differently. Read Betty Edwards – *Drawing on the Right Side of the Brain* and start drawing.

Day 3. Ask and it is given

The universe doesn't understand words, it only responds to vibrations. What kind of energy are you sending out? Begin the journey of clearing out your inner gunk so that you can become a hollow bell. Start to activate your creative muscles by re-framing your perceptions. Chime.

Day 4. Go with the flow

Carry a notebook. Start writing. Anything. Anywhere. No censoring. If you do this quickly, your inner critic won't be able to get a word in edgeways. Remember fast, furious and focused! If you're not familiar with "morning pages" read Julia Cameron *The Artist's Way*. Write.

Day 5. Perception is projection

Our perceptions change slowly as we become more aware. There is no silver bullet, no instant transformation. It takes time to uncouple from our projections. No more whining. Think different.

Day 6. If you love someone, let them go

As soon as you embark on a creative journey, everything you need to let go of will come to the surface and make itself known. Get tough. Name your obsession. Mark 1 or Mark 2 addictions? Meet your Victim archetype and stare it down. Commit to victory.

Day 7. I am an innocent man

Practice feeling happy. Notice your default setting for feeling guilty. Loosen up. Play. Meet your Child archetype and let it off the hook.

Day 8. Get out of your own way

Start clearing up your seven energy centers. Get familiar with your chakras. Break down the silos and free the hostages. We need all this trapped energy for creativity.

Day 9. If it hurts it isn't love

Become aware of how you can be bought and the many ways you negotiate your creative power to another person. Read Chuck Spezzano *If it Hurts it isn't Love*. Meet your Prostitute archetype and re-negotiate terms.

Day 10. Leadership requires humility and an iron will

Shape up or ship out. Meet your Saboteur archetype and shock it into submission with your newfound levels of self-discipline. Practice living with paradox. Creativity requires both focus and fluidity.

Day 11. Know Thyself

Start to reflect on your roles and personalities and the subtle ways these differ from the raw talent of your inner essence. Notice the tendency to control your creative spirit and the need to "own" your soul gifts.

Day 12. Who would I be without my story?

What story are you telling with these roles? Start dissecting the script you've been living your life by. Read anything by Caroline Myss, but for archetypes and the stories they inhabit *Sacred Contracts* is particularly relevant.

Day 13. The map is not the territory

Gain mastery over your emotions. Instead of running away, or being a victim at the side of the hurricane, practice diving into the center of it. Get past the drama of emotions to the deeper feeling underneath. Creative power requires core strength, not the adrenaline of the outer edge.

Day 14. Live in the now

Creativity lives in the now moment. Notice the way you send your spirit on missions to the past (regret and nostalgia) or the future (fear and speculation). Make a decision to channel that energy into something new, different and above all, creative.

Day 15. The universe is abundant

Learn to trust! Stop trying to control your world. Remember Mao Tse-Tung and his sparrows – control is crazy and leads to famine. There is no shortage of creativity, once we deal with our lack of trust.

Day 16. Don't sweat the small stuff

List all your creative traps. Complete the sentence "I'll be creative when... " Either do the stuff or don't do it – as long as you give up thinking about doing it. Notice the amount of time and energy spent just resisting the "stuff of life". It'll always be there, but you can form a different relationship to it.

Day 17. Surrender

We can't think our way to creativity. We have to surrender into it. If we refuse the challenge to live creatively, life can become painful.

Day 18. Step up to the plate

Gain traction at the higher ground. Practice integrating the left and right side of the brain. Check your relationship to rules and the desire to control. Check your relationship to feelings and the aversion to being controlled. Increase your capacity to hold the tension of opposites.

Day 19. Let go of your father

Start looking at the subconscious blocks on the left - the projection that authority figures or bullies patrol the path to creativity. Question the belief you won't survive financially if you give full expression to your creative spirit.

Day 20. Let go of your mother

Start looking at the subconscious blocks on the right - the projection that neediness and vulnerability accompany acts of surrender. Get curious about the world beyond the five senses. Question your fear of abandonment.

Day 21. What you resist persists

Stop fighting and dissociating! End the polarity of "trying to get" and "throwing away". Get curious about what lies between these two.

Day 22. All you need is trust, and a little bit of pixie dust

Start playing with the energy. Believe in magic. Practice *being* the magical, creative child, instead of hanging out with creative people (thereby negotiating your own) or supporting the creativity in others (and sacrificing your own).

Day 23. Everything will be ok as soon as you are ok with everything

Stop fighting. Don't get mad get even. Confront the shadows created by the increased light of creativity by channeling your inner wicked witch into more conscious choices.

Day 24. He not busy being born is busy dying

Let go of what no longer serves you so there is more space for the new to emerge. Practice holding this empty space – it's the dynamic tension between what is and what has yet to arrive. Create the best circumstances in which to birth your creative self.

Day 25. You gotta roll with the punches

Birth is a slow process. Build the strength required to deal with depression, and the courage to handle disappointments with good grace. Develop a patient, waiting attitude. The left-brain likes to rush to the destination in a straight line. The right-brain prefers a zig zag approach, to take advantage of serendipitous events and factor in greater levels of complexity.

Day 26. Breathe

Don't forget the small stuff. Conscious breathing is essential and helps with the discomfort that frequently accompanies dynamic tension.

Day 27. I'll get by with a little help from my friends

Get a support group together. Creativity thrives in the company of like-minded people. Put your hands into something gooey – cake mixture or clay, it doesn't matter. Talk, laugh, brainstorm, play.

Day 28. Who was that masked man?

Practice mashing up your senses to break the stranglehold of the limited structures of the left-brain. Paint a sound. Feel a line. Dance a word.

Day 29. Absorba the Greek

Start to remember the stories that resonated for you at a young age. Begin matching the pattern of these stories to beliefs that you have formed about creativity. How were the heroes and heroines of these stories rewarded for their creative endeavors?

Day 30. Intimacy

In anticipation of high voltage creativity, it is wise to check balancing skills. The neediness vs. control of the Damsel and the Knight. The fear vs. trust of the Orphan and the Magical Child. Good balancing skills will enable you to contain the energy when it arrives.

Day 31. Going back to my roots... yeah

Don't forget the body! It's a great ally in the fight against the supremacy of the mind. Listen to your body and notice if it wants to move (highly likely). Do something physical and rhythmic. Walk, run, dance. Movement is soothing to the spirit and seems to lull the mind into a stupor.

Day 32. We are one

We don't just need creativity for ourselves; we need it for the world! Resist the urge to watch life through the media (and thereby succumb to gossip and opinion.) Life is not a spectator sport. Connect to others and commit to bringing your creativity to the world.

Day 33. We're in the middle of a chain reaction

We are no longer impressed by physical strength or mental prowess; our increasingly complex problems will only be solved with higher levels of creativity. It's the new currency... and not before time.

Day 34. Home is where the heart is

Test your integrated mental skills and your increased emotional strength by taking on the challenge of your family of origin. Stakes are raised now. Love trumps rebellion.

Day 35. Thunderbolt and Lightning very, very frightening... me

Delve further into the unconscious world to discover your deepest fears.

Day 36. It's different for girls

Rescue your female side. Forgive your acts of self-betrayal. Reclaim your creativity. It's time for Scottie to remove the shields.

Day 37. I look at my watch it says 9.25...

Develop a different relationship to time and space. The serendipity of Kairos time and the presence that comes from fully inhabiting the space you're in.

Day 38. Into the mystic – the skinny on the true feminine

Turn up your ability to trust to max power. Revisit the four archetypes of survival and check how they're doing. No more answers. Fall in love with the questions. Fall in love with the mystery of life. Fall in love with being.

Day 39. True grit – the skinny on the true masculine

Turn up your capacity for action. No more adrenaline fuelled fixing of problems, just high voltage creativity channeled into audacious, visionary solutions.

Day 40. Love yourself

At the end of the day, when you get rid of everything that's blocking the flow of energy, there is only love.

And love creates.

Have fun.

HEADLINES

1. Make mistakes.

2. Draw.

3. Chime.

4. Write.

5. Think different.

6. Commit to victory over your addictions.

7. Play.

8. Be aware of your energy system.

9. Value yourself.

10. Exercise discipline.

11. Differentiate between your personalities and your inner essence.

12. Examine your story.

13. Center yourself.

14. Practice living in the now.

15. Trust.

16. Refuse to be sidetracked by the small stuff.

***

17. Surrender into the subconscious.

18. Integrate – hold the dynamic tension of left and right.

19. Fully own your subconscious fears of scarcity.

20. Fully own your subconscious fears of abandonment.

21. Notice your behavior.

22. Become magical.

23. Fully own your subconscious anger.

24, Integrate – hold the dynamic tension of above and below.

25. Build stamina in the waiting game.

26. Breathe.

27. Make friends – consolidate learning.

28. Mash up your senses.

***

29. Surrender into the unconscious.

30. Gain greater balancing and centering skills.

31. Run.

32. Reach out – connect to the world.

33. Contribute.

34. Test your increased inner strength.

35. Go even deeper.

36. Claim your creativity.

37. Live in the now.

38. Meet the true feminine.

39. Meet the true masculine.

40. Meet yourself.

Lightning Source UK Ltd.
Milton Keynes UK
UKHW02f0606050718
325255UK00006B/255/P

9 780956 970800